AI And Law Amid Ethical AI Trends

Advanced Series On
Artificial Intelligence (AI)
And Law

Dr. Lance B. Eliot, MBA, PhD

ISBN: 978-1-95-738607-2

DEDICATION

To my incredible daughter, Lauren, and my incredible son, Michael.

Forest fortuna adiuvat (from the Latin; good fortune favors the brave).

CONTENTS

Note: Visuals are collected together in Appendix B, rather than being interjected into the chapter contents, for ease of reading, enhanced flow, and to see the visuals altogether.

ACKNOWLEDGMENTS

I have been the beneficiary of advice and counsel by many friends, colleagues, family, investors, and many others. I want to thank everyone that has aided me throughout my career. I write from the heart and the head, having experienced first-hand what it means to have others around you that support you during the good times and the tough times.

To renowned scholar and colleague, Dr. Warren Bennis, I offer my deepest thanks and appreciation, especially for his calm and insightful wisdom and support.

To billionaire and university trustee, Mark Stevens and his generous efforts toward funding and supporting the Stevens Center for Innovation.

To Peter Drucker, William Wang, Aaron Levie, Peter Kim, Jon Kraft, Cindy Crawford, Jenny Ming, Steve Milligan, Chis Underwood, Frank Gehry, Buzz Aldrin, Steve Forbes, Bill Thompson, Dave Dillon, Alan Fuerstman, Larry Ellison, Jim Sinegal, John Sperling, Mark Stevenson, Anand Nallathambi, Thomas Barrack, Jr., and many other innovators and leaders that I have met and gained mightily from doing so.

Thanks to Ed Trainor, Kevin Anderson, James Hickey, Wendell Jones, Ken Harris, DuWayne Peterson, Mike Brown, Jim Thornton, Abhi Beniwal, Al Biland, John Nomura, Eliot Weinman, John Desmond, and many others for their unwavering support during my career.

Thanks goes to the Stanford University CodeX Center for Legal Informatics and the Stanford University Computer Science department for their generous support, and for the insightfual and inspirational discussions and feedback from my many fellow colleagues there.

And most of all thanks as always to Lauren and Michael, for their ongoing support and for having seen me writing and heard much of this material during the many months involved in writing it. To their patience and willingness to listen.

CHAPTER 1
INTRODUCTION TO AI AND LAW

This book provides a series of crucial essays encompassing the burgeoning field of AI and the law.

These essays are ostensibly standalone and do not require any prior familiarity with the AI and law topic. You are welcome to read the essays in whichever order you might prefer. The essays have been numbered and sequenced as chapters for ease of referring to the discussions and not due to any need to read one before another.

The essays provide a helpful overview and entry point into the field of AI and law. You will find the essays relatively easy to read and eschew arcane techno-terminology, aiming to layout the vital aspects in clear language and seeking to be readily grasped. The chosen topics entail the latest and hottest trends in the AI and law arena.

For those of you that are potentially interested in knowing more about AI and the law in a deeper way, you might consider my two other books on this subject:

- *"AI and Legal Reasoning Essentials"* by Dr. Lance Eliot
- *"Artificial Intelligence and LegalTech Essentials"* by Dr. Lance Eliot

Those are more akin to textbook-style orientations to the AI and the law field. Both books are available on Amazon and at major bookseller sites. The first book listed provides a comprehensive and detailed exploration of AI and law, while the second book tends to focus primarily on LegalTech and the blending of AI.

One of the most frequent questions that I get asked during my webinars, seminars, and college courses about AI and the law consists of what the phrase "AI and the law" actually refers to.

That's a fair question and deserves a useful answer. In a moment, I will borrow from my other books to provide an explanation about the meaning of "AI and the law" and then dovetail into a brief indication about each of the essays contained in this collection.

Per the essays, you'll end up seeing that there is a great deal of enthusiastic spirit for AI and the law, and likewise a sizable dollop of angst and trepidation about the intertwining of the two. In my view, whether you love it or hate it, there is no stopping the steamroller moving ahead that is going to infuse AI together with the law.

I would urge that any lawyer worth their salt ought to be learning about AI and the law. This will assuredly be especially important for those that are just now starting their legal careers, which I mention because the odds are that the convergence of AI and the law will have an especially pronounced effect throughout your lifelong legal efforts.

For those of you that might be going a more so academic route in the legal realm, rather than being a practitioner of the law per se, the beauty of AI and the law is that there is ample room for new research and a grand opportunity to make a demonstrative mark on the field.

Despite the fact that the field of AI and the law has been studied for many years, dating back to the beginning of the AI field itself, please be aware that we have only scratched the surface on this interweaving. Anyone with a desire to push the boundaries of these two realms will readily find plenty of rampways to do so.

If you are curious about the possible research avenues to pursue, make sure to take a look at my book on *AI and Legal Reasoning Essentials* since it provides a solid foundation on the research to-date and postulates what might be coming down the pike in future research activities. I bid you welcome to the field and wish you the best of luck in your endeavors.

AI And Law

In my viewpoint, Artificial Intelligence (AI) and the field of law are synergistic partners. The intertwining of AI and Law can generally be categorized into two major approaches:

- **AI as applied to Law**
- **Law as applied to AI**

Let us consider each of those two approaches.

AI As Applied To Law

AI as applied to law consists of trying to utilize AI technologies and AI techniques for the embodiment of law, potentially being able to perform legal tasks and undertake legal reasoning associated with the practice of law. Those scholars, experts, and practitioners that have this focus are using AI to aid or integrate artificial intelligence into how humans practice law, either augmenting lawyers and other legal professionals or possibly replacing them in the performance of various legal tasks.

Crafting such AI is especially hard to accomplish, problematic in many ways, and there have been and continue to emerge a myriad of attempts to achieve this difficult goal or aspiration. The rise of LegalTech and LawTech, which is modern digital technology used to support and enable lawyers, law offices, and the like throughout the practice of law are gradually and inexorably being bolstered by the addition of AI capabilities.

There are many indications already of this trend rapidly expanding in the existing and growing LegalTech and LawTech marketplace. Notably, the potent AI and LegalTech/LawTech combination has been drawing the rapt attention of Venture Capitalists (VCs). According to figures by the National Venture Capital Association (NVCA), the last several years have witnessed VC's making key investments of over one billion dollars towards law-related tech startups, many of which have some form of an AI capability involved.

Most of the AI developed so far for LegalTech and LawTech is only able to assist lawyers and legal professions in rather modest and simplistic ways. For example, AI might speed-up the search for documents during e-discovery or might enhance the preparation of a contract by identifying pertinent contractual language from a corpus of prior contracts.

Where the field of applying AI to law is seeking to head involves having AI that can perform legal minded tasks that human lawyers and other legal professionals perform. In essence, creating AI systems that can undertake legal reasoning. This is commonly referred to as AI for Legal Reasoning (AILR).

In a sense, legal reasoning goes to the core of performing legal tasks and is considered the ultimate pinnacle as it were for the efforts to try and apply AI to law. It is undoubtedly one of the most exciting areas of the AI-applied-to-law arena and one that holds both tremendous promise and perhaps some angst and possible somber qualms.

Law As Applied To AI

The other major approach that combines AI and law focuses on the law as applied AI. This is an equally crucial perspective on the AI and law topic.

Sometimes this is also referred to as the **Governance of AI**, though there are those that believe that to be a somewhat narrower perspective on the topic. In any case, the focus is primarily on the governance of AI and how our laws might need to be revised, updated, or revamped in light of AI systems.

You likely already know that AI is experiencing quite a resurgence and has become a key focus of the tech field, along with gaining attention throughout society. AI is being rapidly infused into a wide variety of industries and domain specialties, including AI in the financial sector, AI in the medical domain, and so on.

This rapid pace of AI adoption has opened the eyes of society about the benefits of AI but also has gradually brought to the forefront many of the costs or negative aspects that AI can bring forth. Some assert that our existing laws are insufficient to cope with the advances that AI is producing.

Thus, the need to closely examine our existing laws and possibly revamp them for an era and future of ubiquitous AI.

Expected Impacts

Let's consider how AI and the law can impact those in the AI field, and also contemplate how it can impact those in the field of law.

If you are an AI specialist, you should certainly be interested in the AI and law topic, either due to the possibilities of advancing AI by discovering how to leverage AI into the legal domain or due to the potential of how existing and future laws are going to impact the exploration and fielding of AI systems.

If you are a lawyer or legal specialist, you ought to be interested in the AI and law topic too, for the same reasons as the AI specialist, though perhaps with some added stake in the game.

What is the added stake?

If AI can ultimately become advanced enough to practice law, there is concern by some that it could potentially replace the need for human lawyers and other human legal-related law practitioners.

Some liken this to the famous and telling remark about commitment as exhibited via a chicken and a pig. A chicken and a pig are walking along and discussing what they might do together, and the chicken offers that perhaps they ought to open a restaurant that serves ham-n-eggs. Upon a moment of reflection, the pig speaks up and says that if they did so, the chicken would only be involved (making the eggs), while the pig would end-up being fully committed (being the bacon).

In that sense, AI specialists in this topic are involved, while legal specialists and lawyers are committed.

Meanwhile, for those of you squarely in the field of law, lest you think that AI specialists are to be spared the same fate of being overtaken by AI, you will be perhaps surprised to know that there are efforts underway to craft AI that makes AI, such as in the field of Machine Learning (ML), a specialty known as AutoML, which could potentially put human developers of AI out of a job.

What is good for the goose is good for the gander. Or, it might be that what is bad for the goose is equally bad for the gander.

About These Essays

Now that you've gotten an initial synopsis regarding the topic of AI and law, let's take a moment to briefly take a look at the essays assembled for this decisive collection.

Chapter 1 – Introduction To AI And Law

Key briefing points about this chapter:

- This book is a collection of crucial essays about AI and the law
- The essays are provided as numbered chapters (the sequence is not essential)
- AI and the law consist of two key facets
- One facet is AI as applied to the law (a mainstay of this collection)
- The other facet is applying the law to AI (i.e., governance of AI)

Chapter 2 - AI & Law: Programming Languages

Key briefing points about this chapter:

- There is a lot of attention toward devising apps for legal tasks
- You can use so-called no-code tools, low-code tools, and full-code tools
- Underneath or sometimes on top of things is the programming language being used
- We must ascertain what legal-domain functions such programming languages need
- The rise of AI-in-the-law also has significant ramifications for these matters

Chapter 3 - AI & Law: Family Law

Key briefing points about this chapter:

- A legal marriage would seemingly consist of two persons coming together
- Lawyers versed in family law are quite versed in such legal matters
- Legal researchers are asking whether marriage laws might need some adjustment
- In particular, legally allowing the marriage of a human and an AI-based robot
- Your reaction likely ranges from disbelief to mirth, but some take this seriously

Chapter 4 – AI & Law: Red Teams

Key briefing points about this chapter:

- Computer systems are exceedingly under cyber-attack these days
- Preparation of a computer system ought to include figuring out its vulnerabilities
- A means to discover vulnerabilities consists of using an outside trusted team of attackers
- The use of such teams, known generically as red teams, has become a best practice
- Red teams need to be used on AI systems too, including and especially AI in the law

Chapter 5 - AI & Law: Incident Database

Key briefing points about this chapter:

- AI continues to be a juggernaut of use within modern-day apps and systems
- But AI also has seedy *AI For Bad* issues that are gradually becoming widely known
- A debate is underway about whether to establish a national AI incidents database
- This might seem like an obvious and helpful way of tracking adverse AI
- Not everyone thinks so, and there are lots of legal issues to be dealt with

Chapter 6 - AI & Law: Collective Action

Key briefing points about this chapter:

- AI is amidst many of today's computer systems that we use or encounter daily
- There are unfortunately *AI For Bad* issues, which gradually is becoming uncovered
- Some would say that we are inundated with irresponsible AI development
- This might be seen as a collective action problem that needs to be solved
- Let's consider the legal and ethical AI underpinnings for reaching socially optimal AI

Chapter 7 - AI & Law: Recursion

Key briefing points about this chapter:

- AI in the law can be construed as a two-sided coin
- There is AI applied to the law, simply phrased as AI-Law (hyphenated conjunction)
- There is the law applied to AI, simply phrased as Law-AI (hyphenated conjunction)
- They are able to be considered individually, yet also can be in a repetitive series
- You can think of this as the trendy rinse and repeat, or a form of recursion

Chapter 8 - AI & Law: Federal AI Testbed

Key briefing points about this chapter:

- AI continues to be put into use that at times embeds untoward biases and inequities
- Especially alarming is AI used by our federal government that likewise has such issues
- One proposed approach entails the establishment of an AI-testbed operation
- The AI-testbed operation would be government-run and serve to green light AI systems
- We are still in the early stages of such proposals and details are being worked out

Chapter 9 – AI & Law: Latest Trends

Key briefing points about this chapter:

- Several key trends in AI and law are noted
- A series of levels of autonomy are being devised to aid in differentiating the AI aspects of legal reasoning
- Attorneys with AI-savviness will be able to readily make use of AI in the practice of law
- A relatively new role is emerging known as the legal engineer
- Lawyers ought to be considering learning about AI including how it will change the nature of the legal profession

Chapter 10 - AI & Law: Corporate Governance

Key briefing points about this chapter:

- AI continues to be put into use that at times embeds untoward biases and inequities
- This can end up being the case for all sorts of business AI applications
- In particular, corporate governance systems that embody AI are equally susceptible
- Corporate governance systems would have especially high risks due to their positioning
- Regulatory disclosures laws might need to explicitly mention AI as subject to disclosure

Chapter 11 - AI & Law: Pharm Companies

Key briefing points about this chapter:

- AI continues to be put into use that at times embeds untoward biases and inequities
- A variety of approaches are being floated to curtail or mitigate these AI woes
- One proposed approach is to treat AI makers akin to pharmaceutical firms
- This seems sensible at first glance
- Turns out that the devil is in the detail and the approach might not hold water

Chapter 12 - AI & Law: AI Dev Race

Key briefing points about this chapter:

- AI advancement is rapidly occurring and has generated intense interest all-told
- Some in society are preoccupied with an endpoint of AI becoming sentient
- This is perhaps imprudent and we ought to consider intervening endpoints
- There are also theories that AI development will be discontinuous versus continuous
- All of those considerations have a direct bearing on AI in the law

Chapter 13 – AI & Law: AI Worst-Case Scenarios

Key briefing points about this chapter:

- AI advancement is rapidly occurring and has generated intense interest all-told
- There is an increasing realization that AI can be used for dour purposes
- A poll of AI experts revealed six worst-case scenarios about today's AI
- These are realistic portrayals and not some kind of wide-eyed viewpoint
- We examine each of the worst-case scenarios from a legal and ethical AI mindset

Chapter 14 – AI & Law: China Prosecutorial AI

Key briefing points about this chapter:

- AI advancement is rapidly occurring and has generated intense interest all-told
- For those in the AI-in-the-law realm, AI is being increasingly used for legal tasks
- An AI system in China is reportedly been put in place to make prosecutorial decisions
- In particular, the decision of current focus is about whether to file charges or not
- We examine the nature of this AI and the tradeoffs in such legal usage

Chapter 15 - AI & Law: GDPR XAI

Key briefing points about this chapter:

- AI advancement is rapidly occurring and has generated intense interest all-told
- We are finding ourselves at the whim of AI-based decision-making algorithms
- It is reasonable to expect that the AI would explain its decisions (known as XAI)
- Efforts to craft AI-related regulations and legislation should include such provisions
- The GDPR provides legal language related to XAI and can be handily leveraged

Chapter 16 – AI & Law: Data Poisoning

Key briefing points about this chapter:

- AI is increasingly being used throughout societal applications
- This is partially attributed to the advent of Machine Learning and Deep Learning
- These AI techniques tend to require lots of data for training purposes
- Someone nefarious can attempt to add foul data to confound the AI
- Coined as data poisoning, we examine the legal and ethical AI impacts

Chapter 17 - AI & Law: Adversarial Attacks

Key briefing points about this chapter:

- AI is increasingly being used throughout societal applications
- This is partially attributed to the advent of Machine Learning and Deep Learning
- A cybersecurity ploy to undercut the AI consists of adversarial example attacks
- Someone nefarious can attempt to confound or inappropriately trigger the AI
- We examine the legal and ethical AI impacts

Chapter 18 - AI & Law: Responsible AI

Key briefing points about this chapter:

- AI is increasingly being used throughout societal applications
- Unfortunately, a lot of AI is getting devised that entails *AI For Bad*
- Such AI exhibits racial biases, gender biases, and other inequities
- One means to cope entails pairing attorneys with AI developers
- The gap between them needs to be lessened, aiming to have AI-savvy lawyers

Chapter 19 - AI & Law: Map Of Path Ahead

Key briefing points about this chapter:

- AI in the law is gaining speed and increasingly being applied to many legal uses
- Usual ways of applying AI include e-Discovery, doing legal contracts analyses, etc.
- Some lawyers are behind the times and either ignoring the advent of AI in the law or believe it irrelevant to them
- The ABA has passed a resolution associated with the importance of attorneys being cognizant of AI aspects
- To some degree, you could argue that knowing about AI and the impacts thereof are a duty of being an attorney

Chapter 20 - AI & Law: Robo-Judges XAI

Key briefing points about this chapter:

- AI is increasingly being used throughout societal applications
- In the legal field, there is an ongoing exploration of having AI robo-judges
- There are a slew of tradeoffs about whether to use AI robo-judges or not
- One concern is that seemingly robo-judges won't have sufficient explainability
- There are nuances to this contention that need to be put on the table

Chapter 21 - AI & Law: AI As Board Member

Key briefing points about this chapter:

- AI is increasingly being used throughout societal applications
- Suppose that AI becomes advanced enough to serve in human-like roles
- In particular, envision AI becoming a board member of a corporation
- We can postulate about the legal ramifications of this radical notion
- It is quite unlikely in the near term but worthy of legal exploration anyway

Chapter 22 – AI & Law: Formal Verification

Key briefing points about this chapter:

- AI is increasingly being used throughout societal applications
- Much of the AI is being pell-mell rushed into being fielded
- A lack of dutiful verification and validation (V&V) is widespread
- Lawyers are going to be brought in and asked to deal with unsavory AI
- We provide herein a brief overview of formal verification in the computing realm

Chapter 23 - AI & Law: Differential Privacy

Key briefing points about this chapter:

- AI is increasingly being used throughout societal applications
- This is partially attributed to the advent of Machine Learning and Deep Learning
- These AI techniques tend to require lots of data for training purposes
- The data used for training might get "memorized" by the AI
- An adverse result could be that the AI violates strict privacy laws

Chapter 24 - AI & Law: Disruptive Impacts

Key briefing points about this chapter:

- AI is increasingly being used throughout societal applications
- Many depict AI as being a disruptive technology
- The impression perhaps being a big-bang form of disruption
- A more measured view posits a handy three-part framework
- We explore this in AI business adoption and corporate law impacts

Chapter 25 - AI & Law: Stealing Machine Learning

Key briefing points about this article:

- AI is increasingly being used throughout societal applications
- Much of this AI is based on Machine Learning and Deep Learning
- Suppose someone opts to reverse engineer the AI
- They could set up their own version (cheaply, quickly) or attack the AI
- Significant legal and ethical AI concerns arise

More About This Book

For anyone opting to use this book in a class or course that pertains to these topics, note that Appendix A contains suggestions about how to use the book in a classroom setting.

Furthermore, Appendix B contains a set of slides that depict many of the salient points made throughout the book.

In some of my prior books, I've interspersed the slides into the chapter contents, but feedback by readers has generally been that readers prefer to not have the textual flow become disrupted by the slides, and instead prefer to have the supplemental material assembled altogether into an appendix.

To make sure that you are aware of those added materials, you'll notice that the ending of each chapter provides a quick reminder about the visual depictions that are available in Appendix B.

And so, with this overall orientation to the nature and structure of this book in mind, please proceed to read the essays and learn about the field of AI and law. I'm truly hoping that you'll find the essays mentally engaging and stimulative to the nature of how the law is being practiced and what the future of the law might become.

Note: *For supplemental materials depicting the aspects discussed in this chapter, refer to Appendix B, which contains various augmented diagrams, charts, and additional related facets of relevance.*

CHAPTER 2
AI & LAW: PROGRAMMING LANGUAGES

Key briefing points about this essay:

- There is a lot of attention toward devising apps for legal tasks
- You can use so-called no-code tools, low-code tools, and full-code tools
- Underneath or sometimes on top of things is the programming language being used
- We must ascertain what legal-domain functions such programming languages need
- The rise of AI-in-the-law also has significant ramifications for these matters

Introduction

Suppose that you want to develop an app that will perform some kind of legal task.

How would you do so?

Turns out that there are lots of options, though each option has its own particular tradeoffs.

Some believe that your best bet would be to go with the exceedingly modern-day *no-code* route. In essence, rather than using a programming language at all, you would utilize a software tool that somewhat takes care of the programming for you. These are software packages that tend to be graphical or visually based portrayals of computer-based actions. You use the graphical icons on a drag-and-drop basis. Once you've selected, connected, and devised the sequence of operations, voila, the tool generates a program for you.

For lawyers that want to do programming related to legal tasks, the notion of a no-code solution seems quite inviting. You don't need to learn to code. Toss aside those worries about understanding the in's and out's of some arcane programming language. Instead, you use a graphical interface and merely piece together a legal task running program based on choosing various icons and such.

Well, the reality is that the no-code approach is not entirely a bed of roses. Generally, there are limitations as to what you are able to programmatically produce. You are pretty much boxed in by whatever the no-code solution provides. I'm not knocking no-code. I'm just emphasizing that you should be mindful and cautious in comparing what is possible in no-code versus via more elaborate programming approaches.

Every tool has got to know its limitations, as they say.

Now that we've discussed no-code, our next candidate would be to explore low-code options. These are often akin to no-code but that allows some open-ended capacities to also embed or augment the legal task automation via some semblance of programming code. There can be a bit of a blur between no-code and low-code, depending upon where you wish to draw the line.

The next category would be to proceed with a bonafide programming language.

That's usually the overarching notion behind the lawyers-as-coders refrain.

A begging question is whether it is worth the effort, time, and energy of a lawyer to get up-to-speed in doing programming. Presumably, the lawyer ought to be earning their dough via performing billable legal services hours. Having your head down on programming would seem askew of what an attorney is supposed to be doing. Critics would go further insist it is a travesty, whereby every iota of legal advisory capacity should be devoted to aiding society in legal matters, rather than being "wasted" on everyday programming of code.

Some lawyers relish programming. Good for them, if that's what they wish to do. Others fret that those attorneys are fooling themselves and denying themselves greater riches by trying to write code. It is as though those coding attorneys are caught up in a gold rush of sorts. They have picked up an ax and a pick to mine for gold in those mountains and streams, yet will come away having gotten virtually nothing and be worse off for the eureka fool's errand escapade.

Setting aside whether attorneys should or should not be doing programming, let's shift our attention to a wholly different perspective.

What kind of programming language, if any, would behoove us toward fashioning automation that befits legal tasks in particular?

The idea is that we want to craft a programming language that would be specifically suited for the programming of legal tasks. You see, most programming languages are of a general nature. You can write code that is used for just about any kind of task, such as financial tasks, medical tasks, games, and so on. Versus using a general programming language, we might be a leg up if we had a kind of specialized programming language built from the ground up for the particulars of coding for legal tasks.

I've covered this topic in my writings aplenty.

Part of the reason that I've often discussed the topic is due to the intersection of AI and AI-in-the-law.

We'll come back to that aspect in a moment.

Meanwhile, for ease of discourse, let's refer to a programming language that is a full-blown programming language for legal tasks as its target domain will be known as a full-on coding option (this convenience of naming will help to distinguish it from the low-code and no-code options).

Programming Language Needs

In a research paper entitled "Computational Law: Law That Works Like Software" that was authored by Hans Andersson, the author proffers this statement about programming languages and legal tasks: "The present paper proposes that computational law—law that works like software— systems needs language designed and standardized specifically for legal domains. Any such language system we should build to realize the following desiderata: (1) independence, (2) correctness, (3) expressiveness, (4) determinacy, and (5) (a) succinctness, and (b) usability."

One quick aside about this handy proclamation. You could argue that the identified characteristics or desiderata are equally applicable to a full-code, low-code, and no-code toolset. In other words, the importance of having a programming tool that embodies independence, correctness, expressiveness, determinacy, succinctness, and usability could all ostensibly be applied to whatever kind of legal task programming capability you happen to be assessing. I mention this so as to clarify that those facets are not somehow limited to only the full-code style of possibility.

I realize you might be wondering what those particular characteristics signify in the context of a programming language. I'm glad you asked.

Per the research paper:

- "1. We will call a language system 'independent' iff the system requires no additional language system(s) to practice computational law."

- "2. We will call a language system 'correct' iff the responses it computes from given inputs reflect the responses at which legal professionals would arrive given identical inputs."

- "3. We will call a language system 'expressive' to the extent that we can translate ordinary legal documents into the language system without sacrificing correctness, such that inputs to our translation produce the outputs we would expect to get were we manually to consider the same inputs beneath the ordinary legal documents."

- "4. We will call our new language 'determinate' iff a given program always generates the same responses to the same inputs."

- "5. Finally, we will call our new language (a) 'succinct' and (b) 'usable' iff legal professionals— not necessarily geniuses of software engineering—can represent legal texts and answer legal questions through the use of (a) short programs (b) without difficulty, either mental/conceptual or technical, substantially more than the difficulty that such legal professionals face in the traditional practice of law."

As an aside, the afore indicated quotes include the use of "iff" within them. You might not know that "iff" refers to the logical proposition of something being true "if and only if" its conditions are met on a biconditional basis. Thus, either both statements are said to be true, or both statements are said to be false when interconnecting them with the handy iff.

Due to space constraints herein, I won't weigh in on the desiderata, though I do readily indicate that each such factor is worthy of attention. I bring them to your awareness since they are quite meaningful and important for any programming language that might be devised for trying to encompass legal tasks of one kind of another.

I promised earlier that I was going to tie this into the topic of AI and AI-in-the-law.

Glad to do so. I'd like to make sure to straighten out what it means to refer to AI-in-the-law. I say this because many are often taking a lopsided or narrow view of what the realm consists of.

Please know that there are two major ways to intertwine AI and the law: (1) AI as applied to the law and the practice of law, (2) Law as applied to the advent of AI.

In the first instance, lawyers and legal scholars emphasize the use of AI as applied to the law, which I'll signify as the so-called robo-lawyer, robo-judge, robo-juror, and the like kinds of aspirations. Note that I am not a fan of that robo verbiage, but it is admittedly a quick way to invoke the imagery of what applied AI is ultimately aiming to do.

The second instance consists of applying the law to AI, such as ascertaining how our laws and regulations should be adjusted or crafted anew to cope with the burgeoning use of AI throughout society. This is construed as using legal acumen to figure out the appropriate means of governing AI.

Conclusion

This mentioning of AI and AI-in-the-law is directly pertinent to the programming languages topic that we've earlier been discussing.

Here's why.

Some would argue that we will have AI systems that will perform legal tasks, ergo the implication is that perhaps we won't need any programming languages for legal task implementations. The AI will take care of that for us. If you buy into that logic, you can junk the whole topic of programming languages and also toss into the can the full-code, low-code, no-code debates.

That seems a bit optimistic with regard to the AI side of things.

For example, we will presumably need something to aid us in programming the AI per se. The AI isn't going to simply materialize out of thin air. As such, you could seemingly persuasively argue that any programming language for entailing legal tasks ought to also include facilities related to composing AI capacities.

Another variant would be an AI-based tool that generates code for you. In that manner of thinking, the AI might be used in say a no-code package to do an enhanced job of generating the code for the legal task that you are seeking to program via a graphically oriented user interface.

However you want to look at the matter, the odds are that we will need some manner of programming languages for advancing the use of automation in the legal domain. If that's the case, we ought to also then be identifying what such a programming language needs to contain, making sure that we are armed with the right widgets and facilities to sufficiently aim at the efforts involved in legal tasks and legal reasoning, AI included too, of course.

Note: *For supplemental materials depicting the aspects discussed in this chapter, refer to Appendix B, which contains various augmented diagrams, charts, and additional related facets of relevance*

CHAPTER 3
AI & LAW: FAMILY LAW

Key briefing points about this essay:

- A legal marriage would seemingly consist of two persons coming together
- Lawyers versed in family law are quite versed in such legal matters
- Legal researchers are asking whether marriage laws might need some adjustment
- In particular, legally allowing the marriage of a human and an AI-based robot
- Your reaction likely ranges from disbelief to mirth, but some take this seriously

Introduction

I now pronounce you man and wife.

We all know that famous line.

In many jurisdictions, make that also the possibility of man and man, or woman and woman, or really the phrasing is probably akin to existing California law that entails succinctly stating that it is a person and a person. Thus, I now pronounce you person and person (in terms of being married) as the more applicable wording in those jurisdictions that have such laws.

In California, the legal definition of marriage is officially stated as a personal relation arising out of a civil contract between two persons. Note that consent alone does not generally constitute a marriage, such that there has to be an issuance of a license and a solemnization undertaken.

Other requirements must also be met. For example, the persons must be unmarried, and they must each be an age of 18 years or older. And so on.

Of course, the states differ in terms of their requirements and ergo a plethora of stipulated indications exist regarding what legally qualifies as a state-approved and formalized marriage. Likewise, countries beyond the U.S. also have their own particular ways of legally denoting what marriage consists of. You could say that getting married in any particular jurisdiction across the globe can be like a box of chocolates, meaning that you don't know what their legal viewpoint is about marriage unless you look it up.

In brief, there isn't any singular grand standard about the legal aspects of marriage that everyone has agreed to.

If you closely parse the legal language involved, it would seem that there is one aspect that might nearly be universal about the legalities of getting married. The word that comes to mind is *persons*. Laws are pretty much shaped around the notion that a marriage consists of persons.

I suppose that might seem obvious.

Persons marry persons.

What else would or could they marry?

A recent research article by Ammar Younas, Visiting Professor at the Tashkent State University of Law, indicates that there have been apparently legally approved marriages between a human and a tree in some countries: "Marrying with a tree or tree marriage which symbolizes the marital union of a person with a tree and is said to be infused with supernatural life has long been practiced in different parts of the world. Tree marriage has also been used as a form of proxy marriage in different cultures" (as noted in "Redefining Family: Introducing The Case For Humanoid Robotics In Family Law Jurisprudence In Central Asia").

If that surprises you, get ready for another jolt. Younas also describes marriage in 2013 that took place between a woman and a bridge (taking place in France). Reportedly, this was legally on the up and up (that is almost a bridge-related pun, barely so).

I bring up these facets about marriage to suggest that family law might be heading toward an intriguing disruption of sorts. The rather mind-boggling notion is that perhaps people will seek to legally marry something other than persons, namely aiming to marry AI-based robots.

Farfetched?

Assuredly, it is going to take quite a shakeup in our existing laws, and equally a shakeup in our existing mores and culture, for an extension of the law as going from two persons being eligible to be married and extend into the seeming sci-fi realm of a person and an AI-based robot getting legally betrothed.

You might be rolling your eyes and insistent that no such kind of legal marriage is going to happen. If someone thinks they want to marry an AI-based robot, we might as well open the door to marrying your toaster or your refrigerator. In essence, once you step outside the person's arena, you seem to widely open Pandora's box and the legal world will be thrown for a loop.

One perspective on this ostensibly controversial topic is that it is absurd on the face of the matter and does not warrant any iota of legal discussion or attention. Put the whole thing away. Bring it back out if somehow in the distant future we arrive at sentient AI-based robots. Until then, this is just a bunch of legal shenanigans.

Not so, comes the retort or counterargument.

Even though today's AI-based robots are admittedly not sentient, there is still a case to be made that a robot of contemporary quality is far more than a toaster.

You might have seen on the news about robots that are made to look somewhat like humans, similar to what you might see at a theme park that uses animatronics for their human-looking robots in rides and such. These robots appear to have a head, eyes, ears, mouth, and potentially a human-like body that includes limbs that move and can do some amount of physical exertion.

When infused with today's best AI software, the robot almost takes on an aura or flavor of being human. That being said, let's be absolutely clear about the inarguable fact that none of these robots are at all akin to a human being from a cognitive reasoning capability. I don't care what those eye-catching headlines blare, there isn't any AI today that approaches sentience. On top of that, we don't know when or if we will ever achieve such AI.

In any case, Younas emphasizes that contemporary AI-based robots can still garner human desire for legally being married to the contraption (or, perhaps better stated as contrivance): "It is not astonishing at all if a human falls in love with a humanoid robot since they not only resemble the human body, but it is also very easy to install emotions, to make their skin sensational and to feed them with information which could potentially make someone happy by entertaining them."

Before we get much further into this intriguing topic, let's first discuss the nature of AI and in particular how AI dovetails into the field or domain of law.

Legal Marriages Of Human And Robot

Please know that there are two major ways to intertwine AI and the law: (1) AI as applied to the law and the practice of law, (2) Law as applied to the advent of AI.

In the first instance, lawyers and legal scholars emphasize the use of AI as applied to the law, which I'll signify as the so-called robo-lawyer, robo-judge, robo-juror, and the like kinds of aspirations. Note that I am not a fan of that robo verbiage, but it is admittedly a quick way to invoke the imagery of what applied AI is ultimately aiming to do.

The second instance consists of applying the law to AI, such as ascertaining how our laws and regulations should be adjusted or crafted anew to cope with the burgeoning use of AI throughout society. This is construed as using legal acumen to figure out the appropriate means of governing AI.

Let's noodle on this for a brief moment.

Much of the flashy aspects about AI-in-the-law stems from the application of AI into the law (that's the first case indicated above).

Especially popular ways of applying AI in the law consist of infusing Natural Language Processing (NLP) capabilities into the arduous chore of doing e-Discovery (i.e., AI-based NLP is especially useful when dealing with large-scale narrative-oriented datasets that require extensive and otherwise laborious by-hand legal discovery efforts). And you are perhaps familiar with the use of AI for aiding in examining and composing legal contracts. There are lots of these infusions taking place of plopping AI techniques and technologies into the carrying out bona fide legal tasks.

I'd almost bet that you were probably thinking of AI-in-the-law as purely the application of AI to the law.

Time to expand that way of thinking.

Get ready for the next boon, namely the need to apply the law to AI. This is gradually gaining notable ground and outstretched headlines. Why so? This is partially due to the rampant and uncontrolled promulgating of AI that has showcased seedy and untoward capacities. The recent era of AI began with a rousing cheer that AI would be abundantly good for society, but quickly discovered that there is the grimy underbelly of AI too. AI systems are now suspect right away, often embedding contemptible biases in factors such as race, gender, etc. As a result, the applying of the law to AI is garnering a lot of steam.

Conclusion

Of the two ways to mix together AI and the law, this extraordinary case of legality surrounding a human marrying a robot would clearly fall into the camp of applying the law to AI.

The question on the table is this: *Should our existing laws about marriage be revisited and readjusted to accommodate humans that might want to marry an AI-based robot?*

I know this seems laughable and unworthy of precious lawyering mental cycles.

Maybe this oddish variant of matrimonial pairing is not in the cards for the U.S., at least not for the foreseeable future. On the other hand, we might decidedly witness other countries opting to jump into this legal foray. One supposes that if a person can legally marry a tree or legally marry a bridge, the potential of marrying an AI-based robot ought to be given equal weight.

You could try to go further and make the legal case that a marriage to an AI-based robot is actually more sensible and bona fide than likewise doing so to a tree or a bridge. The AI-based robot can appear to talk and interact (right now, this is on the same level as today's Alexa or Siri). Depending upon the mechanical aspects, the robot might be able to stand up, sit down, walk, run, and carry out other human-like physical movements.

That seems to put the AI-based robot on a closer positioning to a legally allowed marriable "person" than does a tree or a bridge.

Not wanting to put too big of a kibosh on the human-and-robot marriages, but one really pressing issue on the minds of most lawyers and legal scholars is whether or not the AI-based robot can pass the test of agency. So, set aside the tree and the bridge, and instead focus on whether the robot has the appropriate muster to be placed anywhere within the ballpark of human capacities of any salient agency.

The answer right now is that there isn't an AI that comes remotely close to agency in the semblance of human agency. I've discussed this at great length in my writings. As you might imagine, the agency issue comes up repeatedly about trying to nail down the types of new regulations and laws that can sufficiently regulate AI systems.

Anyway, if you are the kind of lawyer that likes to be ahead of the curve, I'm guessing you would relish diving into the future of family law and how this venerated legal domain might change due to advances in AI capabilities. Not only would family law contend with the act of marriage, but Younas also posits that a lot more would legally arise: "A human-robot marriage in the future would pose challenges to lawmakers including whether a human-robot marriage has a legal worth, and how those families will deal with children, property, and issues related to liabilities."

A final twist that maybe seems apparent but in any case is worth mentioning.

Where there are marriages, there are also bound to be divorces too.

Everyone knows (especially lawyers) that where there are laws about marriages, there are bound to be laws about divorces. For those of you seeking to specialize in family law encompassing legal marriages of humans and robots, you ought to be anticipating the subsequent secondary wave of those humans and robots seeking legal divorces.

Catch the first wave, and make sure to be ready for the second wave.

A last thought, a bit of whimsy. Replacing that proverbial and updated refrain that *I now pronounce you person and person* (as in being married), might later include *I pronounce you person and robot.* Which in turn might produce the outsized exhortation, "I want a divorce!" (as said by presumably the human or even by the AI-based robot).

Note: *For supplemental materials depicting the aspects discussed in this chapter, refer to Appendix B, which contains various augmented diagrams, charts, and additional related facets of relevance.*

CHAPTER 4
AI & LAW: RED TEAMS

Key briefing points about this essay:

- Computer systems are exceedingly under cyber-attack these days
- Preparation of a computer system ought to include figuring out its vulnerabilities
- A means to discover vulnerabilities consists of using an outside trusted team of attackers
- The use of such teams, known generically as red teams, has become a best practice
- Red teams need to be used on AI systems too, including and especially AI in the law

Introduction

Sometimes you have to think like the enemy.

In the instance of preparing for a legal case, the usual advice entails putting yourself into the shoes of the opposing counsel. What arguments are they going to make?

Furthermore, what kind of counterarguments will they proffer regarding the legal arguments you are stridently going to produce?

I realize that referring to the opposing side as the enemy is a bit overstated since the notion of an enemy seems perhaps overly harsh, but in some overall sense, you could suggest they are actively opposed or directly hostile to your legal position and accordingly constitute an enemy-like flavor. Maybe we should be softer in our wording and refer to them as your adversary.

This notion of thinking like an enemy or an adversary is well-known in the cybersecurity realm.

Whenever you build or field a computer system that might come under cyberattack, you ought to try and figure out beforehand the potential vulnerabilities that might get exploited by bad hat actors. One way to discern the weak points of your system would be to pretend that you are an attacker of your own system.

A problem with attacking your own system is that you oftentimes will overlook subtle openings that manage to escape your own purview. You are absolutely sure that you've protected against the obvious and the non-obvious, yet this leads you astray as a pretending attacker. A smidgeon of overconfidence and a dash of familiarity tends to block your willingness to go all out and try obscure attacks that might seem useless or pointless. Of course, those seemingly unlikely attacks might be the very ones that a true attacker discovers and gleefully exploits.

What you need to do is make use of trusted outsiders to do the attacking for you, under your careful guise and without them going berserk in their exploitations.

This strategy is undertaken via the use of so-called *red teams*.

Red teams are a commonly used means of having cyber-attacks done at your bidding, being carried out by someone you've employed to do the attacking. These contracted outsiders typically provide a set of fresh eyes at where your system is going to be likely undermined.

The goal that you give them is to go all out and find any viable means of undercutting your system. That being said, you usually hold the line in terms of asking that they don't say take money from your system or fully perform an attack in the manner that a bad actor would. The focus is to find flaws and report them to you, such that you can then adjust or fix your system to be better protected.

I would dare say that nearly anyone in the tech arena knows about the usefulness of red teams. Overall, using red teams would be reasonably proclaimed as an accepted and abundantly acknowledged best practice.

In the same breath, there is something that might be a shocker to you, namely that few AI systems are being tested via the use of red teams. Yes, those zillions of newly built and frantically released AI apps are typically hitting the streets without much in-depth assessment of their exploitable vulnerabilities. This means that there are plenty of AI systems that are ready for the taking by malicious actors that relish using a plethora of cyberattacks.

Gradually, inexorably, a bit of soberness is settling in and the AI world is warming up to using red teams.

As succinctly stated in a recent article published in *Science*: "To address concerns of misuse and new vulnerabilities, a growing number of AI developers are turning to 'red teams'; professionals who consider a system from the perspective of an adversary to identify exploitable vulnerabilities, which can then be mitigated. To date, AI red teams exist mostly within the large industry and government labs, though experts also engage in 'red team' activity in academia and through consultancy" (in an article dated December 10, 2021, entitled "Filling Gaps In Trustworthy Development Of AI" by Sharar Avin et al).

Before we get much further into this intriguing topic, let's first discuss the nature of AI and in particular how AI dovetails into the field or domain of law.

Red Teams Enter Into AI In The Law

Please know that there are two major ways to intertwine AI and the law: (1) AI as applied to the law and the practice of law, (2) Law as applied to the advent of AI.

In the first instance, lawyers and legal scholars emphasize the use of AI as applied to the law, which I'll signify as the so-called robo-lawyer, robo-judge, robo-juror, and the like kinds of aspirations. Note that I am not a fan of that robo verbiage, but it is admittedly a quick way to invoke the imagery of what applied AI is ultimately aiming to do.

The second instance consists of applying the law to AI, such as ascertaining how our laws and regulations should be adjusted or crafted anew to cope with the burgeoning use of AI throughout society. This is construed as using legal acumen to figure out the appropriate means of governing AI.

Let's noodle on this for a brief moment.

Much of the flashy aspects about AI-in-the-law stems from the application of AI into the law (that's the first case indicated above). Especially popular ways of applying AI in the law consist of infusing Natural Language Processing (NLP) capabilities into the arduous chore of doing e-Discovery (i.e., AI-based NLP is especially useful when dealing with large-scale narrative-oriented datasets that require extensive and otherwise laborious by-hand legal discovery efforts). And you are perhaps familiar with the use of AI for aiding in examining and composing legal contracts. There are lots of these infusions taking place of plopping AI techniques and technologies into the carrying out bona fide legal tasks.

I'd almost bet that you were probably thinking of AI-in-the-law as purely the application of AI to the law.

Time to expand that way of thinking.

Get ready for the next boon, namely the need to apply the law to AI. This is gradually gaining notable ground and outstretched headlines. Why so? This is partially due to the rampant and uncontrolled promulgating of AI that has showcased seedy and untoward capacities. The recent era of AI began with a rousing cheer that AI would be abundantly good for society, but quickly discovered that there is the grimy underbelly of AI too. AI systems are now suspect right away, often embedding contemptible biases in factors such as race, gender, etc. As a result, the applying of the law to AI is garnering a lot of steam.

Conclusion

We can now tie together in a tidy bow the aspect of red teams as they pertain to AI in the law.

First, anyone that is applying AI to the law should be sufficiently giving due consideration to the use of red teams.

Once you've got your AI-infused LegalTech app or system somewhat underway, you would be wise to make use of a red team to attack it. This will hopefully reveal any residing vulnerabilities. Those vulnerabilities could have undermined the AI once it got into production and possibly wreaked havoc accordingly, especially so in whatever legal context the AI-in-the-law system is designed to befit.

Second, the other side of the coin entails the law as applied to AI, as mentioned earlier, and thus we need to also identify how red teams can be construed in a legal milieu.

For example, if you have a client that has allegedly been harmed by an AI system, did the developers of the AI perform due diligence and make use of a red team? Those AI systems that haven't undergone a red team assessment could be said to open the door to legal woes as a result of not taking sufficient precautions related to their AI app.

On a related aspect, some believe that our laws pertaining to AI should strictly stipulate that red teams are to be used. There would be various caveats associated with this stipulation, such as perhaps based on the size, magnitude, and nature of the AI system. The idea would be to find a balance between using red teams (which can be costly) versus averting red teams simply by default penny-pinching or by outright omission.

There you have it, the red teams approach as applicable to AI in the law. You see, thinking like the enemy (or, shall we say adversary) might be a helpful and welcomed means of trying to cut down on the *AI For Good* that keeps getting overturned into becoming *AI For Bad.*

Note: *For supplemental materials depicting the aspects discussed in this chapter, refer to Appendix B, which contains various augmented diagrams, charts, and additional related facets of relevance.*

CHAPTER 5

AI & LAW: INCIDENT DATABASE

Key briefing points about this essay:

- AI continues to be a juggernaut of use within modern-day apps and systems
- But AI also has seedy *AI For Bad* issues that are gradually becoming widely known
- A debate is underway about whether to establish a national AI incidents database
- This might seem like an obvious and helpful way of tracking adverse AI
- Not everyone thinks so, and there are lots of legal issues to be dealt with

Introduction

There is a brewing brouhaha underlying the proposed formulation of a national AI incidents database.

Plenty of legal and ethical AI issues are intertwined with this quite serious and strident matter. You might have assumed that there shouldn't be anything of notable controversy on such a topic, but that is decidedly not the case. Verbal fisticuffs are both quietly and at times loudly being employed.

Let's unpack things.

Just a few years ago there was a palatable sense of excitement that AI was advancing sufficiently to provide some valuable capabilities for modern-day apps and systems. The buzz was entirely about the advantages of *AI For Good*, meaning that AI could contribute potentially toward solving various thorny problems confronting society. Soon thereafter, the thrill somewhat wore off as people began to experience *AI For Bad*, such as AI-based facial recognition that exhibited racial biases and other disquieting AI-powered inequities.

One question that has arisen deals with whether we ought to be adequately kept informed about AI that has inadvertently gone astray or perhaps even has been *purposely* devised to generate *AI For Bad* consequences. The most often proposed means by which we would be looped in on such shenanigans would be via the establishment of a national AI incidents database.

The concept is that whenever AI is caught being untoward, an incident would be logged in the national AI incident database. We would all then presumably be able to know which AI has gone bad in some manner and ergo be on our toes that the particular AI should be considered less trustworthy.

Inching Toward A National AI Incidents Database

This kind of national-oriented incidents database all-told is not a new idea per se. In fact, some argue it is an old hat.

Take for example the National Transportation Safety Board (NTSB) and their national-focused database concerning aviation incidents. The database is an NTSB maintained log of aviation incidents, including data about when the flight incident occurred, the severity of the adverse outcome, type of aircraft, who was operating the aircraft, and so on. Few would seemingly argue in opposition to this NTSB flights-oriented incidents database. More so would tend to applaud it and emphasize the value of the database to society.

Another akin example of a national incidents database is one that you probably haven't heard of, unless perchance you work in the tech field, namely the CVE (Common Vulnerabilities and Exposures). The CVE is quite well-known amongst programmers and nearly any type of computer-related developer or high-tech company.

The idea is pretty simple, keep track of cyberattacks and other computer-based vulnerabilities that arise, logging them into an accessible incidents database. A federal agency on cybersecurity oversees the database and receives funding from the U.S. Department of Homeland Security.

Okay, you now should ostensibly be convinced that having national incident databases is a legitimate affair (I've cited two examples, plus there are many more out there). If we already accept that national incident databases are a suitable and sensible concoction, it would seem as easy as falling off a log to assume we should do the same for AI-related incidents.

You might brashly say, case closed.

Not so fast, the retort or counterargument exhorts.

One confounding issue is that though we can readily get our arms around circumstances such as when an aircraft incident occurs or when a computer system breach happens, the same clarity cannot be said about so-called AI incidents.

What would constitute an AI incident?

You just opened an entire can of worms. The notion of what would be subject to logging in to a national AI incidents database is undoubtedly going to drag the whole shebang into both a legal and ethical AI quagmire.

First, there assuredly would need to be a legally defined understanding of what is AI and what is not AI. I've discussed in my writings that there is an existing legal vagueness when it comes to defining AI. The regulatory definitions are rife with problems. At times, the definition of AI is overly narrow and would allow AI-salient systems off-the-hook, in a manner of speaking, while in other instances the definition is so broad that just about any computer app or system would suddenly become "AI" and require being logged.

Second, there would need to be teeth behind any stated requirements to report on AI incidents, else the odds are that many relevant or on-target AI-related incidents would be swept under the rug and not see the light of day. What kinds of legal penalties of either a criminal or civil nature would be imposed for those that aren't willingly notifying about their AI incidents occurrences?

Third, what would be the characteristics of an incident worthy of being logged? An obvious factor would be if the AI-led to physical harm, producing injury or death. Less obvious and yet still demonstrative would be something along the lines of transgressions regarding fairness, accountability, and transparency (FAT). Unfortunately, there are a lot of loosey-goosey facets that could curtail or undercut those at times less quantifiable or tangibly provable considerations.

And so on.

Some suggest that we might not need hard-and-fast legal stipulations. Perhaps the ethical AI aspects would be enough to get AI incidents reported. Organizations that fail to report their AI incidents might be the butt of societal scorn. Also, employees within such organizations might ethically feel betrayed by the firm and become a whistleblower or might vote with their feet by leaving the firm and causing a sizable talent drain.

How are we to proceed with figuring out the modalities of a national AI incidents database?

The approach underway right now seems to be of a stepwise nature, putting our toes gently at first into the AI incident's rocky waters.

You see, the existing aim toward the establishment of a national AI incidents database involves non-governmental or third-party efforts that some hope will gradually turn into a federally produced AI incidents database: "Incident sharing could become a regulatory requirement. Until then, voluntary sharing can be incentivized, for example, by allowing anonymous disclosure to a trusted third party. Such a third party would need to have transparent processes for collecting and anonymizing information and operate an accessible and secure portal" (as stated in *Science*, December 10, 2021, "Filling Gaps In Trustworthy Development Of AI").

A leading example of a third-party proffered AI incidents database is a system called AIID (AI Incident Database) being promulgated by an entity known as the Partnership on AI (PAI). PAI is an organization consisting of public and private corporate companies and non-profit entities, stitched together into a multi-stakeholder framework.

The technical design of the AI incidents database is discussed in an article by Sean McGregor and mentions: "The AIID is a collection of web applications that interfaces with a MongoDB document database storing incident report text and metadata. The first application developed for the database is the 'Discover' application, which is built to help users discover past incidents relevant to their work" (as stated in "Preventing Repeated Real World AI Failures By Cataloguing Incidents: The AI Incident Database").

Per the online website now showcasing the budding AI incidents database of PAI, their taxonomy, such as type of data captured in the AIID includes but is not limited to (at this time):

- Description of the incident (short, full)
- Severity of harm (negligible, minor, unclear/unknown, moderate, severe)
- Uneven distribution of harms basis (race, sex, religion, national origin, age, etc.)
- Harm type (harm to social or political, psychological harm, physical health/safety, civil liberties, financial harm, etc.)
- System developer
- Sector of deployment
- Relevant AI functions (cognition, perception, action, unclear)
- AI tools and techniques used (machine learning, facial recognition, natural language processing, etc.)
- AI functions and applications used (decision support, recommendations engine, autonomous driving, etc.)
- Location
- Named entities
- Dates of incident
- Probable level of intent (accident, unclear, deliberate or expected)
- Human lives lost
- Infrastructure sectors affected
- Total financial cost
- Laws covering the incident
- Level of autonomy (unclear/unknown, low, medium, high)
- And various other factors

Conclusion

Some final remarks for now.

Please know that there are two major ways to intertwine AI and the law: (1) AI as applied to the law and the practice of law, (2) Law as applied to the advent of AI.

In the first instance, lawyers and legal scholars emphasize the use of AI as applied to the law, which I'll signify as the so-called robo-lawyer, robo-judge, robo-juror, and the like kinds of aspirations. Note that I am not a fan of that robo verbiage, but it is admittedly a quick way to invoke the imagery of what applied AI is ultimately aiming to do.

The second instance consists of applying the law to AI, such as ascertaining how our laws and regulations should be adjusted or crafted anew to cope with the burgeoning use of AI throughout society. This is construed as using legal acumen to figure out the appropriate means of governing AI.

This discussion about an AI incidents database is principally on the side of the coin dealing with applying the law to AI. If private efforts to generate an AI incidents database are to be gradually transformed into a federally maintained national one, there is going to be a lot of lawyering needed to get us there.

Plus, you can bet that whatever is put in place will likely face legal objections by firms that don't necessarily want to get logged, or that get logged and try to fight the government to be removed from the AI incidents database. There are bound to be lots of outcrying clients seeking law firms for particular legal assistance regarding any kind of federally maintained AI incidents database.

Not wanting to leave untouched the other side of the coin, which consists of AI applied to legal tasks, this will turn out to also get mired in any AI incidents database considerations. For example, a law firm is using an AI-based LegalTech software tool to aid in some aspect of lawyering, and suppose that the tool turns out to have or somehow incurs an alleged AI incident-pertinent facet.

Now what?

Well, presumably, the AI incident ought to get logged into the (let's assume) federally maintained AI incidents database. The law firm might be aghast at being mentioned in such a database. The vendor of the AI-based LegalTech tool might also be upset that their software is logged in the AI incident database.

The odds are that the earlier point of legally fighting against the AI incident database would entail.

For lawyers, it seems that no matter which way you opt to view the matter of an AI incidents database, the legal world is going to be engaged.

Note: *For supplemental materials depicting the aspects discussed in this chapter, refer to Appendix B, which contains various augmented diagrams, charts, and additional related facets of relevance.*

CHAPTER 6
AI & LAW: COLLECTIVE ACTION

Key briefing points about this essay:

- AI is amidst many of today's computer systems that we use or encounter daily
- There are unfortunately *AI For Bad* issues, which gradually is becoming uncovered
- Some would say that we are inundated with irresponsible AI development
- This might be seen as a collective action problem that needs to be solved
- Let's consider the legal and ethical AI underpinnings for reaching socially optimal AI

Introduction

There continues to be a daily revealing of both expected and unexpected ways in which AI is acting quite untoward these days.

To clarify, I am not suggesting that contemporary AI is somehow autonomous or sentient. Instead, I am referring to the increasing realization that the techniques and technologies underlying the development and fielding of AI are frequently prone to producing systems that embed a plethora of societal wrongdoing.

We have gradually witnessed AI that exhibits racial biases, gender biases, and a slew of other inequities. You can also add safety risks to the concerns about AI, including the potential for AI to go off the rails and cause bodily harm.

Some would woefully argue that we are currently in a fierce battle between *AI For Good* and *AI For Bad*, for which the adverse side of AI seems to be gaining traction.

Of course, all of this is AI that is based assuredly on what AI developers are opting to do. You cannot try to be tricky or do a false wink-wink and say that AI will do as AI will do. People are developing today's AI. Until we someday, if ever, reach a point of AI that seemingly crafts itself in a completely independent manner, you can still place the root of the badness of AI at the feet of those humans that are proffering such AI, whether they realize they are doing so or not.

What spurs AI developers to code AI systems that have adverse consequences?

An interesting macroscopic perspective is that the nature of this irresponsible AI development and the contrasting shall we say proper goal of seeking responsible AI development are part of a larger-scale problem, namely the so-called *collective action problem*.

Let's unpack that proposal.

Researchers describe the collective action problem related to AI in this manner: "In most industries, private companies have incentives to invest in developing their products responsibly. These include market incentives, liability laws, and regulations. We argue that AI companies have the same incentives to develop AI systems responsibly, although they appear to be weaker than they are in other industries. Competition between AI companies could decrease the incentives of each company to develop responsibly by increasing their incentives to develop faster. As a result, if AI companies would prefer to develop AI systems with risk levels that are closer to what is socially optimal—as we believe many do—responsible AI development can be seen as a collective action problem" (per the paper by Amanda Askell, Miles Brundage, Gillian Hadfield entitled "The Role of Cooperation in Responsible AI Development").

In a nutshell, those producing AI systems are in a frantic race to do so on a first-mover basis. Meanwhile, the societal environment in which this is taking place could be said to be lacking or not keeping up with what is happening. The argument is that there are insufficient laws or regulations to incentivize or penalize those that irresponsibly produce today's AI systems. Other market forces such as ethical AI considerations have also not been sufficiently promulgated to act in a counterbalancing manner to the first-mover urges driving the AI developers.

There is a massive race to the bottom on safety.

You might be wondering why the AI arena should somehow be the only such circumstance of a race to the bottom. Seemingly, the same should be occurring in other industries. Here's what the researchers point out: "We might ask why racing to the bottom on product safety is not ubiquitous in other industries in which decreasing time-to-market is valuable, such as in the pharmaceutical industry. The most plausible explanation of this difference is that the cost of safety failures has been internalized to a greater extent in more established industries via external regulation, self-regulation, liability, and market forces" (per the article by Askell, Brundage, and Hadfield).

What we need to do is cajole, entice, incentivize, and prod the sanctity of responsible AI development, which is defined as: "Responsible AI development involves taking steps to ensure that AI systems have an acceptably low risk of harming their users or society and, ideally, to increase their likelihood of being socially beneficial" (per Askell, Brundage, Hadfield). In the same breath, you could readily argue that we need to stop, curtail, mitigate, and castigate irresponsible AI development. Seems like both a carrot and a stick are warranted.

Five Factors Toward Responsible AI Development

Let's assume for the moment that the legal and ethical AI factors continue to lag.

What then?

Perhaps we simply are to shrug our shoulders and wait until those externalities finally catch up and serve as a boundary-shaping encapsulation to try and ensure AI development of a more responsible kind. Or we might eternally twiddle our thumbs and take our lumps, doing so under the expectant belief that maybe the *AI For Good* is so strongly valued that we regrettably will also endure the *AI For Bad*.

Neither of those options seems especially astute. There ought to be some means to prod AI developers to craft AI systems that are at risk levels of a more societally preferred level, phrased at times as said to be AI of a *socially optimal caliber*.

According to this cited research, we can overcome the collective action problem by purportedly paying attention to five key factors underlying responsible AI development, specifically: "We identify five key factors that make it more likely that companies will be able to overcome this collective action problem and cooperate—develop AI responsibly with the understanding that others will do likewise. These factors are high trust between developers (*High Trust*), high shared gains from mutual cooperation (*Shared Upside*), limited exposure to potential losses in the event of unreciprocated cooperation (*Low Exposure*), limited gains from not reciprocating the cooperation of others (*Low Advantage*), and high shared losses from mutual defection (*Shared Downside*)" (per the article by Askell, Brundage, and Hadfield).

I won't dig into the details herein for sake of brevity (readers are encouraged to explore the research paper for gleaning the underlying particulars).

The overarching argument being made is that by abiding by those five factors, AI developers would tend to find themselves better off, overall, and ergo end up toeing the line toward *AI For Good* and averting the insidious path of *AI For Bad*.

Some specifics to highlight how those five factors might be enacted include (per the authors):

- "Social incentives (e.g. valorizing or criticizing certain behaviors related to AI development) can influence different companies' perceptions of risks and opportunities,
- Economic incentives (induced by governments, philanthropists, industry, or consumer behavior) can increase the share of high-value AI systems in particular markets or more generally, and increase attention to particular norms,
- Legal incentives (i.e. proscribing certain forms of AI development with financial or greater penalties) could sharply reduce temptation by some actors to defect in certain ways,
- Domain-specific incentives of particular relevance to AI (e.g. early access to the latest generation of computing power) could be used to encourage certain forms of behavior."

Conclusion

Some final remarks for now.

Please know that there are two major ways to intertwine AI and the law: (1) AI as applied to the law and the practice of law, (2) Law as applied to the advent of AI.

In the first instance, lawyers and legal scholars emphasize the use of AI as applied to the law, which I'll signify as the so-called robo-lawyer, robo-judge, robo-juror, and the like kinds of aspirations. Note that I am not a fan of that robo verbiage, but it is admittedly a quick way to invoke the imagery of what applied AI is ultimately aiming to do.

The second instance consists of applying the law to AI, such as ascertaining how our laws and regulations should be adjusted or crafted anew to cope with the burgeoning use of AI throughout society. This is construed as using legal acumen to figure out the appropriate means of governing AI.

This discussion about the need to push for responsible AI development is principally on the side of the coin dealing with applying the law to AI. The viewpoint of the collective action problem seems to be that until there are presumably sufficient legal regulations and legal pressure for responsible AI development to be otherwise enforced and perceived as being legally required, we will have a bit of a wild west underway. You can add in a dose of ethical AI conditions too, such that until society brings to bear ethical norms and pressures, the maverick and at times irresponsible AI development will continue to flourish.

Not wanting to leave untouched the other side of the coin, which consists of AI applied to legal tasks, will turn out to also get mired in similar considerations. For example, a law firm is using an AI-based LegalTech software tool to aid in some aspect of lawyering, and suppose that the tool turns out to have or somehow incurs untoward aspects.

This could assuredly occur. The irresponsible AI development has just as much chance of taking place in the legal domain as it does in other domains. You would though tend to assume that AI developers immersed in a legal domain would be aware of the potential onslaught of legal wranglings and lawsuits that would come at them from their very base of users (lawyers and other such legal professionals), but do not hold your breath on that assumption.

Responsible AI development is not guaranteed and we have to be on a vigilant watch to avert succumbing to irresponsible AI development, at all times.

Note: *For supplemental materials depicting the aspects discussed in this chapter, refer to Appendix B, which contains various augmented diagrams, charts, and additional related facets of relevance.*

CHAPTER 7
AI & LAW:
RECURSION

Key briefing points about this essay:

- AI in the law can be construed as a two-sided coin
- There is AI applied to the law, simply phrased as AI-Law (hyphenated conjunction)
- There is the law applied to AI, simply phrased as Law-AI (hyphenated conjunction)
- They are able to be considered individually, yet also can be in a repetitive series
- You can think of this as the trendy rinse and repeat, or a form of recursion

Introduction

Rinse and repeat.

There is a popular meme that ostensibly says to wash, rinse, and repeat. Some prefer to indicate instead that you should lather, rinse, and repeat. That seems indicative of shampooing your hair versus the use of the word "wash" per se that otherwise implies cleaning just about anything.

Given that we relish shortening and abbreviating today's catchy phrases, the most popular variant of this trendy saying has been boiled down to simply stating to rinse and repeat. Of course, this does not mean to actually rinse something, nor does it mean to *repeatedly* rinse something in a literal fashion.

We accept that this phrasing has become a quick and quite fashionable way to indicate when any circumstance or advisory steps have become repetitive or should be performed repetitively.

In the computer field, there is a slightly different means of asserting that you should rinse and repeat. The word recursion is often used to denote an algorithm that repetitively does its actions. A distinctive characteristic typically associated with recursion is that it is the same aspect that gets repeatedly performed and can be at times considered as being woven into levels such that it can later be unwoven from those levels.

Imagine that I am on a forest trek and decide that I don't want to get lost in the woods. Turns out I perchance am carrying a loaf of bread. Each time that I come to a fork in the wooded path, I put down a bread crumb to mark which fork I've taken. I do this repeatedly for several miles of my outdoor adventure. Let's assume I eventually come to a wonderous waterfall, and this is the furthest I wish to venture. What a tremendous view!

I turn around and head back to my car that is parked at the originating point of my trek. By watching for those breadcrumbs that I had left along the trail, I am able to detect which way to proceed. I'll go ahead and pick up the breadcrumbs as I gradually make my way to the parking lot.

In a broad manner of speaking, my algorithm entailed putting breadcrumbs at each fork, doing so repeatedly upon encountering any forks in the trail. I was able to later unwind this procedure and use the breadcrumbs on the reverse course of my journey.

Now, to clarify, you don't necessarily need to do an unwind when you are using recursion. It all depends on how you set it up and whether you wish to undertake a rewind at all. For example, it could be that upon reaching the waterfall, a friend of mine conveniently lands their helicopter nearby and gives me a lift over the top of the forest and returns me to my car (well, that's if I knew someone that perchance flew helicopters, had one and was willing to whisk me out of the woods). In any case, I didn't particularly do an unwind and you could say merely escaped out of the earlier winding.

We will come back to this loosey-goosey definition of recursion in a moment. You'll soon see that it was worth considering.

AI In The Law As A Two-Sided Coin

Shifting gears, let's discuss the rising topic of AI in the law.

You might be surprised to know that this is a bit of a two-sided coin. Please be aware that there are two major ways to intertwine AI and the law: (1) AI as applied to the law and the practice of law, (2) Law as applied to the advent of AI.

In the first instance, lawyers and legal scholars emphasize the use of AI as applied to the law, which I'll signify as the so-called robo-lawyer, robo-judge, robo-juror, and the like kinds of aspirations. Note that I am not a fan of that robo verbiage, but it is admittedly a quick way to invoke the imagery of what applied AI is ultimately aiming to do.

The second instance consists of applying the law to AI, such as ascertaining how our laws and regulations should be adjusted or crafted anew to cope with the burgeoning use of AI throughout society. This is construed as using legal acumen to figure out the appropriate means of governing AI.

Much of the flashy aspects about AI-in-the-law stems from the application of AI into the law (that's the first case indicated above).

Especially popular ways of applying AI in the law consist of infusing Natural Language Processing (NLP) capabilities into the arduous chore of doing e-Discovery (i.e., AI-based NLP is especially useful when dealing with large-scale narrative-oriented datasets that require extensive and otherwise laborious by-hand legal discovery efforts). And you are perhaps familiar with the use of AI for aiding in examining and composing legal contracts. There are lots of these infusions taking place of plopping AI techniques and technologies into the carrying out bona fide legal tasks.

I'd almost bet that you were probably thinking of AI-in-the-law as purely the application of AI to the law.

Time to expand that way of thinking.

Get ready for the next boon, namely the need to apply the law to AI. This is gradually gaining notable ground and outstretched headlines. Why so? This is partially due to the rampant and uncontrolled promulgating of AI that has showcased seedy and untoward capacities. The recent era of AI began with a rousing cheer that AI would be abundantly good for society, but quickly discovered that there is the grimy underbelly of AI too. AI systems are now suspect right away, often embedding contemptible biases in factors such as race, gender, etc. As a result, the application of the law to AI is garnering a lot of steam.

Recursion Steps Into The Picture

For ease of convenience, accept the terminology of using "AI-Law" to indicate the application of AI to the law, and also accept the use of "Law-AI" to indicate the application of the law to AI. Those are hyphenated conjunctions (not to mistakenly be misread as a minus sign form of abstraction).

Consider that each of those sides of the coin can potentially impact the other.

We might apply AI to the law, creating handy AI-based tools for crafting or analyzing our laws. In the next and *subsequen*t breath, we might look closely at the laws so generated or adjusted if they have anything substantive to do with regulating or governing AI.

All told, we can phrase this conveniently like this: **AI-Law : Law-AI**.

There is a similar but switched around version that we can consider too. Clean out your thinking and start fresh. Let's see what we can come up with.

We might apply the law to AI by establishing some new laws to govern or regulate AI systems. Afterward, we might opt to apply AI to the law, though we now would also presumably need to be mindful of whatever laws were created or amended that perhaps encompass the AI that we are building to perform legal tasks.

We can phrase this as: **Law-AI : AI-Law**.

I trust that this all seems sensible and on the up and up.

Wanting to do some rinse and repeat, or invoking a taste of recursion, we can expand on these rudiments.

Mull over this: **AI-Law : Law-AI : AI-Law**.

The interpretation would be that we applied AI to the law, which then dovetailed into our applying the law to AI (we just momentarily earlier covered that), and then this carried over into once again applying AI to the law. That makes indubitable sense. We might have put in place new laws that govern AI, and this led us to adjust or make anew some form of AI-infused LegalTech accordingly.

I suppose you are likely to guess my next iteration.

Ponder this one: **Law-AI : AI-Law : Law-AI**.

You likely can interpret that without any added assistance.

We can continue to extend this series. To be somewhat smarmy about it, you could exhort that we can do a rinse and repeat.

Conclusion

The gist of the discussion is that you should not perceive the two sides of the AI-in-the-law coin as somehow separate and apart from each other and never coming in contact (I suppose that's a downfall of using a coinage metaphor). Each can inevitably and inexorably impact the other.

For that, I'll claim we are using a variant of recursion and avert talking any further about the overused and downtrodden meme of lather, rinse, and repeat.

Note: *For supplemental materials depicting the aspects discussed in this chapter, refer to Appendix B, which contains various augmented diagrams, charts, and additional related facets of relevance.*

CHAPTER 8

AI & LAW: FEDERAL AI TESTBED

Key briefing points about this essay:

- AI continues to be put into use that at times embeds untoward biases and inequities
- Especially alarming is AI used by our federal government that likewise has such issues
- One proposed approach entails the establishment of an AI-testbed operation
- The AI-testbed operation would be government-run and serve to green light AI systems
- We are still in the early stages of such proposals and details are being worked out

Introduction

Suppose you are opting to make use of a governmental service that is available online and uses the latest and greatest in AI technology.

You might be elated and indeed pleasantly surprised that the feds are employing modern-day AI capabilities.

Seems like our governmental pace of adoption entailing new and innovative high-tech often is woefully lagging. Nonetheless, in this particular circumstance, they got their act together and the AI seems as smooth as silk to use.

Turns out that not all is rosy in the land of AI usage.

Later it is revealed that apparently unbeknownst to the federal agency that deployed the AI system, the AI is replete with various sordid biases. There are racial biases ingrained in this particular AI. There are gender biases embedded within it. A plethora of inequities is being essentially fostered and furthered via a federally-used AI system.

Sickening, disheartening, outrageous, shouldn't happen.

Part of the issue is that though AI can proffer some quite handy amenities, it also can harbor ugly and altogether untoward badness. We have gradually come to realize that the touted *AI For Good* has a seedy underbelly entailing *AI For Bad*. You've likely seen the massive headlines about AI-powered facial recognition systems that are exhibiting adverse biases and it seems like each day we learn about other additional AI-related abhorrent problems.

We are likely to find especially egregious instances wherein our own government ends up utilizing AI that is replete with these kinds of issues. If a private company deploys AI that has bad elements, we would assume and expect that the company will suffer a truckload of consequences. When the federal government uses bad AI, we rightfully feel utterly betrayed and were otherwise at the mercy of whatever the trusted agency decided to implement.

Some fervently argue that the government needs to be held to a higher standard of what kind of AI they are building or procuring. Society deserves to be comfortable knowing that the AI employed by the feds will be on the up and up. A special and heightened duty to ferret out any lurking AI badness seems warranted and ought to be obliged.

Proposal For Government-Run AI-Testbed

How would the government attempt to figure out whether the AI they are planning to use or that is already in their use might contain adverse ethical AI or unlawfully performing AI?

Proposed answer: *Make use of a government-run AI testbed.*

The idea is that any federal entity using AI would need to first have the AI screened and get a green light before the desired AI could be placed into active use. All of this examining of the AI would be performed by a dutifully authorized and government-run AI-testbed operation.

Some assert that there should just be one centralized AI-tested operation, while others suggest that there ought to be numerous such operations. Tradeoffs exist as to which way to structure those operations in actual practice.

There is also some debate about whether this AI-testbed validation would always need to be undergone versus whether agencies could decide when they think it is justified to undertake. Proponents of always having to use the AI tested would insist that otherwise, the government will tend to take the lazy route and avoid undergoing the testing. Those that say it should be considered optional are prone to emphasizing that a required usage could unnecessarily delay the adoption of the latest AI systems and merely become yet another bureaucratic stumbling block hampering innovation within the federal arena.

In any case, let's take a look at a recently proposed approach for such an AI-testbed.

One proposal for a government-run AI testbed explains the importance this way: "Increasing federal usage of AI systems, coupled with the vulnerabilities of AI models to internal malfunction and external attack, means that it is of utmost importance to create a testbed for government uses of AI. A testbed, broadly speaking, is typically a facility staffed with subject-matter experts who conduct rigorous evaluations of a certain type of technology using a variety of tools and methodologies. While there are not yet standardized metrics or benchmarks to evaluate what makes an AI system robust or secure, establishing a federal AI testbed will help push the field in the right direction" (as per Tina Huang, Stanford Institute for Human-Centered AI (HAI), *Institute For Progress*, January 19, 2022, "Creating an AI Testbed for Government").

There are additional crucial facets for establishing a federal AI-tested, including: "Such a testbed will help AI researchers and developers better understand how to construct testing methods and ultimately build safer, more reliable AI models. Without this capacity, U.S. agencies risk perpetuating existing structural inequities as well as creating new government systems based on insecure AI systems — both outcomes that could harm millions of Americans while undermining the missions that federal agencies are entrusted to pursue" (per Huang's article).

Keep in mind that the AI-testbed envisioned would be solely devoted to AI systems utilized by the government, either one built by the government or AI systems procured by the government: "This proposal focuses on creating a testbed specifically for government-procured AI systems — from simple rules-based models to models learning from data — that are used to provide services to Americans" (per Huang's article).

As an aside, another open question involves whether the AI would only be subject to the AI-testbed if it was *customer-facing* to those that use governmental services. In essence, if the AI was behind the scenes, it would presumably not need to undergo the AI-tested process.

Hogwash, some say. The worry is that the behind-the-scenes AI could be unduly embedding biases and that the end result would ultimately fall upon those using the governmental services, regardless of whether they had directly interacted with the governmental AI system or not.

As you can likely see, there are lots of devils in the details aspects that will need to get worked out.

Conclusion

You might have already discerned that the proposed AI-testbed is going to raise quite a number of hefty legal questions.

Will we need new laws that would essentially compel government agencies to use the AI-testbed?

Assuming that new laws are so enacted, you can bet that the laws will be at times be skirted or loosely interpreted in a manner that might not comport with what was intended. As such, you can bet that there will be legal skirmishes about the meaning and implementation of the laws.

Imagine too that the AI-testbed is put into use and becomes a legal requirement for federal agencies, but along the way, there are problems (this ought to be expected). The government procures an AI system that successfully passed the AI-testbed. Unfortunately, the AI-testbed missed catching some untoward biases in the AI system. Oopsie. Those that have been harmed in some manner by government-run AI systems would presumably now seek some legal redress for their damages.

Yet another qualm is that the AI that is tested might not be the same as the AI that ends up in day-to-day use. Allow me a moment to explain this.

Some AI can essentially alter itself throughout its usage, especially so-called Machine Learning or Deep Learning. This is generally construed as a type of "learning" by the AI, though I caution against using the word "learning" since it implies a human-like capacity of learning that we ought to not yet be ascribed to today's AI capabilities.

Please do not anthropomorphize the AI of today.

In any case, the AI that let's assume passed with flying colors the AI-testbed might change itself once it has been placed into active use. If you are willing to assume that the AI-testbed found no untoward elements at the time of testing (which, of course, there is not a reasonably viable and altogether practical means to be one hundred percent certain), this might have little to do with the AI after it has been fielded for a while.

I realize that an easy answer would be that the AI ought to have to undergo a form of periodic recertification, but that's not quite as straightforward as you might think. When would the recertification take place? Would it be done soon enough to catch the AI going untoward before it went off the rails? How often and at what cost would this recertification occur? Etc.

One last remark for now.

Another notable complication consists of defining AI per se.

As I've written extensively, there is no concrete singular acknowledged standardized legal definition of what AI is. In that manner of a conundrum, you can ask whether the AI-testbed would be able to appropriately get its arms around which computer systems of the government would need testing and which would not.

An overly broad definition of AI might force all sorts of everyday computer systems of the government to undergo the AI-testbed, potentially overrunning available testing resources and incurring a rather burdensome cost to all concerned. An overly narrow definition of AI would perhaps allow genuine AI to avert being tested by claims of a loophole or other escape hatch.

The one thing you can stridently say about an AI-testbed for governmental systems is that the legal world is going to be needed and a whole lot of legal wrangling is going to arise.

That's for sure.

Note: *For supplemental materials depicting the aspects discussed in this chapter, refer to Appendix B, which contains various augmented diagrams, charts, and additional related facets of relevance.*

CHAPTER 9
AI & LAW:
LATEST TRENDS

Key briefing points about this essay:

- Several key trends in AI and law are noted
- A series of levels of autonomy are being devised to aid in differentiating the AI aspects of legal reasoning
- Attorneys with AI-savviness will be able to readily make use of AI in the practice of law
- A relatively new role is emerging known as the legal engineer
- Lawyers ought to be considering learning about AI including how it will change the nature of the legal profession

Introduction

A lot is going on in the burgeoning intersection of Artificial Intelligence (AI) and the law.

Let's take a quick look at some key trends and cover keystone foundational facets at the same time.

The place to start would be to clarify how AI and the law intertwine. These two fields or domains are synergistically being combined in a seeming multitude of disparate ways.

Headlines tout how AI is coming to the assistance of lawyers in the everyday practical performance of legal work. Meanwhile, new laws are being devised to cope with AI that has seemingly gone off the rails and exhibited untoward biases and inequities. All told, the quick pace and blaring announcements underlying AI and the law can be overwhelming, appearing to be entirely chaotic and without any semblance of coherence.

Turns out that a rather straightforward and handy macroscopic perspective provides a much clearer view of their intermixing. You see, there are two major approaches to combining AI and the law:

(1) **AI-Law** -- *AI as applied to the law and the practice of law,*
(2) **Law-AI** -- *Law as applied to the advent of AI.*

In the first instance, lawyers and legal scholars emphasize the use of AI as applied to the law, which I'll signify as the so-called robo-lawyer, robo-judge, robo-juror, and the like kinds of aspirations. Note that I am not a fan of that robo verbiage, but it is admittedly a quick way to invoke the imagery of what applied AI is ultimately aiming to do.

Much of the flashy aspects about AI-in-the-law stems from the application of AI into the law, especially as AI is progressively being added to contemporary LegalTech systems.

Numerous AI-infused LegalTech offerings now include Natural Language Processing (NLP) capabilities, akin to embellishing legal task-oriented computer software with the interactivity associated with Alexa or Siri. In this case, the NLP is tuned specifically to performing legal work. Other AI techniques and technologies are equally be integrated into LegalTech packages, especially the use of Machine Learning and Deep Learning (popular computational pattern matching capabilities).

Consider some primary examples of AI that is applied to the law.

Lawyers often endure arduous and exhausting energies expended toward doing suitable e-Discovery. The latest NLP paired with e-Discovery tools provides legal professionals with a handy means of inspecting large-scale narrative-laden datasets. This can be done in more fluid legal-like language and queries, rather than the arcane and stilted commands of conventional tech.

Another AI amplified example consists of the lawyering activity when drafting legal contracts. With a properly AI boosted contract life cycle management (CLM) tool, an attorney can have the AI attempt to pull together an initial draft of a contract. At that juncture, the lawyer proceeds to do refinements, saving them the time and attention that would have been needed to start a new contract from scratch.

That briefly covers the realm of AI applied to the law.

The second instance or proverbial *other side of the coin* consists of applying the law to AI.

Legal acumen is required to ascertain how our laws and regulations should be adjusted or crafted anew to cope with the expanding use of AI throughout society. Lawyers are needed that can aid in formulating sensible laws to battle the rise of so-called *AI For Bad.*

You've likely seen that AI systems are being fielded that have inherent racial or gender biases. This can occur for a variety of technical reasons, including that the training data used in Machine Learning and Deep Learning might a priori contain such inequities and the computational pattern matching simply carries these characteristics into the algorithmic decision making (ADM) being fostered.

Besides needing attorneys that are sufficiently savvy about AI for purposes of drafting or passing laws covering AI systems, you can also anticipate that a lot of legal work is going to arise as a direct consequence of releasing AI that has gone astray, getting those daring firms into legally bubbling hot water.

Beyond any doubt, there are going to be a slew of companies that have rashly and rapidly adopted AI into their services or products that will suffer a backlash when the embedded AI turns out to be functioning inappropriately. Lawyers deeply familiar with conventional laws and with AI-specific laws will be sought by those firms.

You can expect that there will be both civil cases and even criminal cases that will be shaped around how AI was devised and put into active use. Some suggest that only the AI will carry the weight of the legal burden, and ergo wring their hands that we need to legally anoint AI with a status akin to legal personhood.

Though there is a lot of wide-eyed talk about AI that somehow works on its own, please know that today's AI is not autonomous and turn your attention to the humans behind-the-scenes that will ultimately be held responsible for the misdeeds of their promogulated AI. Do not fall for the classic distraction that the computer did it, which hasn't (or shouldn't have) worked before and still won't work even with the most advanced AI of today.

This is a judicious segue into some of the latest research and works on AI in the law, consisting of a proposed set of Levels of Autonomy (LoA) associated with AI within the legal field (an area of AI in the law that I've extensively explored in much of my writings).

The notion of autonomous levels is likely something you've heard about, though in an entirely different context. You might be somewhat aware that autonomous vehicles (AV) and particularly self-driving cars are typically depicted by their autonomous levels. An international standard exists that lays out a series of levels of autonomy, starting at the basest level of 0 (no driving automation) and ranging to a topmost level of 5 (fully autonomous driving). Various AI-augmented cars are being tried out on our public roadways that showcase elements of these varying levels of autonomy.

I've sketched a similar layout for the aspects of augmenting legal work with AI. A range of levels of autonomy are described when undertaking AI Legal Reasoning (AILR), namely:

- Level 0: No Automation for AI Legal Reasoning
- Level 1: Simple Assistance Automation for AI Legal Reasoning
- Level 2: Advanced Assistance Automation for AI Legal Reasoning
- Level 3: Semi-Autonomous Automation for AI Legal Reasoning
- Level 4: Domain Autonomous for AI Legal Reasoning
- Level 5: Fully Autonomous for AI Legal Reasoning

Using this framework will aid in discerning the wheat from the chaff, so to speak, when it comes to vendor products and outsized claims about how they have added AI to their LegalTech wares.

Imagine that a vendor comes out with an augmented CLM that claims to have NLP and utilizes Machine Learning, which seems impressive on a cursory basis. Is this a buzzword salad or does it truly provide bona fide traction toward AI being useful in a legal task? We can ask a direct and succinct question to try and gauge what the AI proffers in this context.

What level does this AI provide for the legal task at hand?

Upon undertaking an appropriate rating or assessment, assume that the CLM with AI amplification is classified as being at a Level 2. Therefore, this is considered advanced assistive automation rather than existing as a semi-autonomous or fully autonomous capacity.

Meanwhile, in ready comparison, suppose that a competing vendor has a CLM boosted AI tool that is rated as a Level 3. All else being equal, one can readily construe that the Level 3 product has a superior level of an autonomous facility than the Level 2 offers. Thus, the use of this LoA enables a kind of above-board playing field and readily facilitates head-to-head comparison.

Conclusion

For those of you that are wondering what aspects of AI in the law you ought to be pursuing, I'll provide a bit of quick advice.

First, take a contemplate moment to reflect on your personal and professional interests and goals.

The application of AI to the law is likely to require a heightened semblance of technical prowess. If you are a lawyer or budding lawyer that also relishes high-tech, this would put you in a good posture for becoming involved professionally in AI as applied to LegalTech.

You might also then be interested in considering becoming a legal engineer. This is a relatively new kind of role that will gradually be found in larger law firms and especially in LegalTech vendors. The duties entail being roughly equally capable in the aspects of computing and the realm of the law.

Shifting gears somewhat, the applying of the law to AI is more so a legal-oriented effort, thus you don't necessarily need as much of a bent toward technology per se. You can generally be a lot lighter on the technical underpinnings.

In fact, if you have even a dollop of knowledge about computers and AI, this will almost immediately put you a step ahead of many others in the law that are just now struggling to deal with laws surrounding and engulfing AI. A little bit of AI savviness will take you a long way.

The overall gist is that you hopefully have some altogether passion or keen interest in AI, for which you can then stay at the edges of the technology and partake in the applying of the law to AI, or you can dive in with both feet into AI and tend to focus on the applying of AI to the law.

No matter which path you choose, be assured that the future of the law is going to inexorably be impacted by AI. You are lucky enough to be standing in the infancy of something that will eventually be grandly encompassing.

Note: *For supplemental materials depicting the aspects discussed in this chapter, refer to Appendix B, which contains various augmented diagrams, charts, and additional related facets of relevance.*

CHAPTER 10
AI & LAW:
CORPORATE GOVERNANCE

Key briefing points about this essay:

- AI continues to be put into use that at times embeds untoward biases and inequities
- This can end up being the case for all sorts of business AI applications
- In particular, corporate governance systems that embody AI are equally susceptible
- Corporate governance systems would have especially high risks due to their positioning
- Regulatory disclosures laws might need to explicitly mention AI as subject to disclosure

Introduction

Let's talk about corporate governance.

There seems little doubt that companies are likely to succeed or fail as dependent upon the strength of their top management and as aided by or crucially overseen by their board of directors. The overarching strategy of the firm emanates from those key roles.

If the corporate strategy is askew then the chances are relatively high that the company won't last, faltering and flailing as it desperately tries to stay in business. You could argue that corporate governance is the essential glue or maybe better depicted as the vaunted grease that keeps the top layers of the firm running at needed speeds.

By and large, the work undertaken by top management and its board is bound to be conducted via human-to-human interaction, or so one might assume. This kind of top-level strategizing would certainly seem to require those keen eye-to-eye discussions about what the business should be doing and why so. Handshakes and all that.

The somewhat dour emphasis is that the use of advanced technology to somehow support or even spur the intricate and delicate matters of corporate governance might at first glance seem unlikely and inapplicable. Like the shoe cobbler's children, the top hasn't viewed high-tech as particularly helpful for corporate governance, despite the obvious fact that technology now permeates all other facets of the firm.

That notion of eschewing technology in the capacity of corporate governance enablement is gradually being seen as false, quite old-fashioned, and generally out of touch.

Just like everything else about today's modern corporation there is a great deal of value in making use of or adroitly leveraging technology for nearly all tasks and efforts by the firm. For example, in the case of top management and their board, we certainly likely all agree that at least the use of email, remote online meeting software, and similar electronic communications-oriented high-tech is absolutely necessary and abundantly being used.

Another rising use of tech for corporate governance consists of the board portal or dashboard. The idea is that an electronic single-source of truth gets put in place and provides top management and the board with essential information at their fingertips. Materials are posted into the portal that is then readily accessed and can be electronically shared and discussed.

Some of these dashboards were initially nothing more than a fancy datastore repository. Dump various reports and data into the portal and that's all there was to it. Directors of the company had to sift through it all. Maybe they would happen upon the right stuff or maybe not. Top management would also find themselves at times overwhelmed with the content bloating their revered board dashboard.

Gradually, there was a realization that specially devised computer programs could turn the vast mountain of reports and data into something more intelligible. When board members or top management logged into the portal, they were now greeted with computer-analyzed insights that could be rerun at will. Rather than necessarily relying upon an army of human analysts to cull through the content, executives and directors could do the same by pressing a button or two.

We are now venturing into the logically expected next step on this use of high-tech in the corporate governance realm, namely the addition of AI into the mix.

As you will see in a moment, the use of AI can demonstrably lift the nature of robo-analyses being done for corporate governance purposes. There is also the use of algorithmic decision making (ADM) that facilitates the AI toward potentially "making top business decisions" at the highest levels of the firm and then promulgates those choices throughout the company.

How far should this use of AI take us in the altogether sober and make-or-break seriousness of corporate governance?

Recent headlines wring their hands that we are heading toward a lot of troubles ahead on this particular use of AI. You see, it is AI at the top, which means that whatever it does or doesn't do, and whether it is working properly or inappropriately, can insidiously permeate the rest of the organization, readily so. The AI has been anointed as the top-level last word or inarguable strident command.

You can bet your bottom dollar that AI used in the corporate governance arena will ultimately and inexorably come under intense legal scrutiny. Questions about whether existing laws adequately cope with AI entailing corporate governance will arise. New laws about the application of such AI will be established. And, meanwhile, ethical AI concerns will be rife about how this AI was devised and fielded.

When Corporate Governance Becomes AI Swayed

There is a boatload of so far unvetted qualms about AI in the corporate governance arena.

Researchers rightfully proffer that significant risks are afoot: "Privacy and security issues become important since large amounts of data are fed to the AI system. Even if secure AI systems are developed, relying on judgments made by an AI system has other risks. The 'black box problem' or the lack of transparency with AI decision-making has been flagged in various contexts in which the use of AI has gained prominence. This is likely to be an issue for corporate governance as well. Further, human bias may get embedded within an AI system when it is fed biased data" (per Akshaya Kamalnath and Umakanth Varottil, "A Disclosure-Based Approach To Regulating AI In Corporate Governance" as a *National University of Singapore Law Working Paper*, January 2022).

Board members and top execs can become lulled into believing that the AI is merely telling it like it is. There is a common fallacy that AI is somehow entirely neutral, unbiased, and forthright. If you want to get the real scoop about what is happening in the company, the AI is supposedly going to give you the unvarnished truth.

The rising realization that *AI For Bad* is an underlying and integral other side of the coin for *AI For Good* is opening our mindset about how AI works. We've seen that AI systems can exhibit racial and gender biases, along with fostering an additional slew of inequities.

To clarify, this impudence of the AI is not to suggest that the AI of today is sentient. Please know that there isn't AI that comes even close to sentience at this time and we don't know for sure when this might happen, nor do we know if it will indeed happen at all.

Today's AI is much more down-to-earth, composed by the hands and efforts of humans, and often crafted such that it contains human biases and faults, warts and all.

As stated in the research paper by Kamalnath and Varottil about corporate governance and AI usage: "There is also the more basic problem of AI making mistakes, with black-box decision-making coming in the way of humans obtaining a full appreciation of the reasons for those mistakes. In the corporate governance context, these decisions may have serious consequences which shareholders and other stakeholders of the company may have to suffer. Concomitantly, directors could very well bear the brunt under the current directors' liability framework for manifestations of AI risk. These concerns call for a risk-based assessment of the utility of AI in corporate governance."

In brief, AI at the corporate governance function is replete with potential legal liabilities for board members and top management. There is also the danger of reputational fallout if the AI either directly or indirectly aids in producing a corporate calamity or failure. The researchers suggest that three paths are available to spur realizations that AI might overstep or be allowed to overstep in a corporate governance role: "The typical regulatory options for any issue range from hard law (enforceable rules) to soft law (voluntary guidelines or principles to be followed) to simply doing nothing."

Doing nothing would appear to be the proverbial head-in-the-sand option.

Existing regulatory provisions or hard laws are do not yet explicitly mention AI in the capacity of corporate governance. Disclosures required under most laws today blandly entail that any notably "material" aspects are to be disclosed.

This materiality conception traces to the U.S. Supreme Court ruling of *TSC Industries Inc v. Northway Inc that* stated material information consists of "a substantial likelihood that the disclosure of omitted fact would have been viewed by the reasonable investor as having significantly altered the 'total mix' of information made available" (SCOTUS 426 U.S. 438, 1976).

Upon reviewing various corporate governance regulatory options, the researchers Kamalnath and Varottil recommended that disclosure facets need to be adjusted and amplified to specifically include AI-related salient aspects: "Hence, given the increasing use of AI in corporate governance, there is a strong case for the introduction of specific disclosure norms pertaining to AI. A disclosure-based approach is particularly important at this relatively early stage in the deployment of AI in corporate governance, and before it becomes mature enough for other forms of regulatory monitoring to take hold."

Conclusion

The gist of what needs to be done is that we ought to close the barn door before the horses get out. Rather than waiting to see whether AI-pertinent disclosures are warranted, the belief is that AI encompasses enough hidden risks that it seems a foregone conclusion that AI-specific disclosures are going to be needed regarding corporate governance uses.

Without engaging in a separate debate of a rather heated nature, some would argue that the urgency to include AI is exemplified by the recent spate of required disclosures about climate change. In essence, the argument is put forth that the climate change disclosure requirements were perhaps brought ahead on a belated basis and should have taken hold sooner. Whether you agree or not with that assessment, the point here is that some assert that AI is in the same camp of being something that we cannot wait until further down the path to try and get our hands around.

You might ostensibly be convinced that formalizing AI-related corporate governance disclosures seems like a no-brainer and should be instituted without delay. Not everyone would concur with that sentiment.

Counterarguments abound.

For example, how are we to define what AI constitutes such that it comes under the rubric of any such required disclosures? If the boundaries of AI as a construct are wide, we'll force companies into all sorts of oddball and unneeded disclosures. If the boundaries are narrow, corporations will escape the requirement by merely noting that their software is not AI per se.

Other concerns include that disclosing the AI being used could give away precious corporate proprietary means and methods. This could further reveal the valuable intellectual property of the firm. Some say that the AI disclosures might muddy the waters of the disclosures all told, rendering the disclosure aspects more opaque and confounding or confusing shareholders and other stakeholders. The ruckus over the AI disclosure aspects prompted researchers Kamalnath and Varottil to make this recommendation: "Hence, at this stage, it would be prudent to introduce disclosure norms on a 'comply-or-explain' basis, with sufficient flexibility to companies to determine the content and extent of disclosures."

All told, this is yet another crucial indicator that the introduction of AI into the business world and society, in general, is a matter subject to legal and ethical considerations, whether everyone realizes it or not. Some sage advice would seem to be that it is better to be in the realization mode than caught in the perilous unawares mode.

Note: *For supplemental materials depicting the aspects discussed in this chapter, refer to Appendix B, which contains various augmented diagrams, charts, and additional related facets of relevance.*

CHAPTER 11

AI & LAW: PHARM COMPANIES

Key briefing points about this article:

- AI continues to be put into use that at times embeds untoward biases and inequities
- A variety of approaches are being floated to curtail or mitigate these AI woes
- One proposed approach is to treat AI makers akin to pharmaceutical firms
- This seems sensible at first glance
- Turns out that the devil is in the detail and the approach might not hold water

Introduction

AI keeps rolling along and increasingly appearing in all manner of societal apps and everyday computerized systems.

At first, there was a rallying cry supporting the pell-mell rush toward app makers fervently AI-enabling the widest array of applications.

The belief was that AI infusion would embolden apps that would be much more usable. In a manner of speaking, the software could now meet us halfway toward not being just an app and instead be something uplifted that can seemingly communicate in uncannily intelligible ways. All of this got brightly and gleefully labeled as the emergence of *AI For Good.*

But then the *AI For Bad* began to arise.

You've certainly seen, heard, or even experienced the sour side of AI. Turns out that AI systems were being devised and fielded that contain a slew of sordid biases, including racial bias, gender bias, and other inequities. You've likely seen the massive headlines about AI-powered facial recognition systems that are exhibiting adverse biases and it seems like each day we learn about other additional AI-related abhorrent problems. We have gradually come to realize that the touted *AI For Good* has a seedy underbelly entailing *AI For Bad.*

Sickening, disheartening, outrageous, shouldn't happen.

What are we to do about this untoward AI scourge?

Many are clamoring for new laws that will rein in the *AI For Bad* impetus. There are ongoing debates about whether existing laws are sufficient, thus the legal argument exists that we likely need additional laws that specifically aim at the AI realm. Meanwhile, numerous efforts to raise ethical AI awareness are trying to fill the gap while legal machinations eventually catch up to the bad AI.

Proposal For Treating AI Makers Akin To Pharma

One notable legal-oriented proposal that seems to be garnering attention is to treat AI makers akin to how pharmaceutical companies are legally dealt with.

Specifically, the notion is that AI systems would need to undergo some form of formal and explicitly stipulated scrutiny prior to being released.

If the AI cannot pass muster, it would be prohibited from being let loose. Hefty legal penalties would correspond to anyone not abiding by the legally binding assessments undertaken.

Some legal researchers envision that there would be a specialized group or formal screening body that would do the testing and issue permits or licenses for AI systems. Here for example is one such description of how this process might be employed: "The specialized body in the AI context would have an 'a mixture of technical, ethical, legal and economic expertise'. The body would then aim to ascertain a few criteria including whether there is embedded bias, whether developers of the relevant AI technology were a diverse group, whether public interest is served by the product, and whether the decisions made by the product are explainable." (as mentioned by Akshaya Kamalnath and Umakanth Varottil, "A Disclosure-Based Approach To Regulating AI In Corporate Governance" as a *National University of Singapore Law Working Paper*, January 2022).

In a sense, the idea is that we don't allow new drugs to be willy-nilly brought into the marketplace and ergo we shouldn't let AI be fostered upon the world without first getting properly prescreened. Let's, therefore, go ahead and use what we've learned from the pharmaceutical industry and readily reapply it to the AI domain.

Easy-peasy.

Not so fast, many would counterargue vehemently.

First, a hugely unsettled question is what constitutes AI. As I've previously expounded in my writings, there isn't a single across-the-board standard definition of AI. This is a big problem. If we aren't definitive about what AI is, there is a solid chance that many budding systems that do contain AI can try to skirt around the envisioned testing process. The software makers would insist that they aren't embodying AI into their systems.

If we decide to craft a broad definition of AI to try and ensure we encompass those escapists that would desire to avert the process, the odds are that a lot of relatively non-AI systems would get carried inadvertently into the testing fold. You would have a bottleneck testing process that becomes choked by zillions of software apps having to walk a strict and overbearing gauntlet, perhaps unfairly so.

Another qualm is that the very act of imposing the testing process is going to add significant costs to software development and create unimaginable delays for getting AI into the hands of society. Might we delay innovations that are sorely needed as soon as possible? Some lament that treating AI makers like pharma would pretty much destroy the innovation and fast pace heralded generating of those *AI For Good* systems that are eagerly being sought.

The range and extent of problematic concerns for this pharma-like instantiation are loudly being voiced. You are going to kill the goose that laid the golden egg. You are going to bureaucratize the AI industry. The tech world will presumably rebel, doing so in a powerful way as commensurate with their enormous size and resounding impact on today's society.

As examples of the thorny aspects to be worked out:

- Would the testing be at a centralized location or distributed throughout the country?
- Would the testing be government-run and if so by which agency?
- If the testing is private-run, how will that work, and what controls over it will be instituted?
- Would there be timetables to ensure that the testing is done on a timely basis?
- What recourse would an AI maker have if their AI was assessed as unsuitable for release?
- How would the testing even ascertain the issues being pursued to uncover?
- Would AI developers react by devising trickery to hide and sneak through their apps?

Yet another qualm is that the AI that is tested might not be the same as the AI that ends up in day-to-day use. Allow me a moment to explain this.

Some AI can essentially alter itself throughout its usage, especially so-called Machine Learning or Deep Learning (popular computational pattern matching techniques and AI technologies). This is generally construed as a type of "learning" by the AI, though I caution against using the word "learning" since it implies a human-like capacity of learning that we ought to not yet be ascribed to today's AI capabilities.

Please do not anthropomorphize the AI of today.

In any case, the AI that let's assume passed with flying colors the AI testing might change itself once it has been placed into active use. If you are willing to assume that the AI testing found no untoward elements at the time of testing (which, of course, there is not a reasonably viable and altogether practical means to be one hundred percent certain), this might have little to do with the AI after it has been fielded for a while.

I realize that an easy answer would be that the AI ought to have to undergo a form of periodic recertification, but that's not quite as straightforward as you might think. When would the recertification take place? Would it be done soon enough to catch the AI going untoward before it went off the rails? How often and at what cost would this recertification occur? And so on.

An intriguing twist described by researchers Kamalnath and Varottil is based on the work of Frederick Hayek as noted in his famous article "The Use Of Knowledge In Society" from 1945 (*American Economist Review*). Here's what Kamalnath and Varottil have to say: "Further, the fast pace of innovation in this field means that appropriate laws (for each sector) cannot be enacted in advance of the licensing process. In other words, the model runs into the Hayekian knowledge problem, i.e., where the planners (government or even regulatory bodies) may not have the required information about the activity."

Conclusion

You might have already discerned that the proposed notion of treating AI makers akin to the pharmaceutical industry raises quite a number of hefty legal questions.

Assuming that new laws of that ilk are enacted, you can bet that the laws will be at times be skirted or loosely interpreted in a manner that might not comport with what was intended. As such, you can wager that there will be legal skirmishes about the meaning and implementation of the laws.

All told, the one thing you can stridently say about the treatment of AI makers in a pharma-like manner is that the legal world is going to be needed and a whole lot of legal wrangling is going to arise.

That's for sure.

Note: *For supplemental materials depicting the aspects discussed in this chapter, refer to Appendix B, which contains various augmented diagrams, charts, and additional related facets of relevance.*

CHAPTER 12

AI & LAW: AI DEV RACE

Key briefing points about this essay:

- AI advancement is rapidly occurring and has generated intense interest all-told
- Some in society are preoccupied with an endpoint of AI becoming sentient
- This is perhaps imprudent and we ought to consider intervening endpoints
- There are also theories that AI development will be discontinuous versus continuous
- All of those considerations have a direct bearing on AI in the law

Introduction

Imagine for a moment that you are in a forest and suddenly notice that a bear is eyeing you from behind a thicket of trees.

This is a rather daunting and disheartening situation, for sure.

The age-old question arises as to whether you should stand your ground or run for the hills. If you stay in your existing spot, the bear could presumably dart right at you and the rest is history. If you opt to flee, the problem with that option is that bear might be able to outrun you, plus the act of fleeing could trigger the bear into coming at you. No doubt about it, things are in a bit of a pickle for you.

Suppose that you are with a camping buddy and the two of you are standing next to each other in the midst of this dire predicament. There is a rather coarse witticism concerning this type of quandary. The joke goes like this. Your fellow camper starts to tighten their shoestrings, suggesting that they are going to make a run for it.

You clear your heavy throat and ask your companion whether they think that they can really outrun a bear. It seems dubious and highly risky. Your buddy looks you squarely in the eye and vociferously proclaims that they aren't worried about outrunning the bear. You see, the only feat they have to do is outrun you.

Drum roll ensues.

This quip means that your so-called buddy is willing to leave you behind as bear food. Maybe it is a telltale sign that you should begin putting some serious thoughts toward finding someone more steadfast to go camping with.

We can use this clever snippet to consider some facets underlying the act of running a race. Sometimes the race is timed and your main goal is to finish in the shortest amount of time. In other cases, the race is against a fellow racer and you are primarily aiming to hit the finish line before they do. Of course, you might be paying attention to more than one metric, such that you want to best the other runner and do so in a phenomenal time.

Why do I bring up the inner psychological game of running races?

Because some ardently believe the advent of AI is essentially a running race.

You might have seen splashy headlines that indicate the U.S. is either ahead of or perhaps behind the pace of other countries when it comes to doing AI development. Likewise, the states across the U.S. are often in a race to see which one will garner the most AI developers and be the most productive in generating AI apps.

Companies that craft AI software are equally in a race of sorts. The moment that one company announces a breakthrough in some esoteric element of AI, you can bet that shortly thereafter another competing firm will declare that they too can do the same AI. Furthermore, that competing firm will probably claim that they have gone beyond what the first company proclaimed.

All told, there seems to be a multitude of interlocking and intersecting races toward advancing AI.

For lawyers and those serving as legal scholars, the AI race might at first glance seem not particularly relevant or important to the field of law. Let those AI developers duke it out. The whole one-upmanship gambit is perhaps mildly interesting to law practitioners or legal studiers, but otherwise, it is not worth any rapt attention.

Wait for a second, let's see if that blind eye is sensible or not.

First, let's take a quick look at the nature of AI-in-the-law to lay the groundwork for analyzing the underway and ongoing AI race.

You might be surprised to know that AI-in-the-law is a bit of a two-sided coin. Please be aware that there are two major ways to intertwine AI and the law: (1) AI as applied to the law and the practice of law, (2) Law as applied to the advent of AI.

In the first instance, lawyers and legal scholars emphasize the use of AI as applied to the law, which I'll signify as the so-called robo-lawyer, robo-judge, robo-juror, and the like kinds of aspirations. Note that I am not a fan of that robo verbiage, but it is admittedly a quick way to invoke the imagery of what applied AI is ultimately aiming to do.

The second instance consists of applying the law to AI, such as ascertaining how our laws and regulations should be adjusted or crafted anew to cope with the burgeoning use of AI throughout society. This is construed as using legal acumen to figure out the appropriate means of governing AI.

The Role OF Endpoints When Racing Toward AI

Back we go to the running races.

There is a common misconception that the race toward AI is one that consists of a particular endpoint, namely the attainment of AI arriving at sentience. Perhaps this aspiration is fueled by all those sci-fi movies, or merely part of the outstretched dream of trying to replicate human sentience into a machine.

The idea that AI developers are consumed with producing sentience is farfetched. Sure, there are AI developers that harbor that vaunted goal, no doubt about it. Other AI developers would be ecstatic if somehow they stumbled upon generating AI that was sentient. All in all, almost no one of any measured reasoning about today's AI is under the wistful guise that they are going to produce sentient AI.

In short, we aren't anywhere near that endpoint, and we don't know what it will take to get there. Nobody can say whether we will ever achieve AI sentience.

I bring up the endpoint question due to the confusion over endpoints as a gauge for where AI is and where it will be going next. As this insightful research abundantly makes clear, we need to revisit the false or misleading mantra of an AI totality endpoint: "Much of the discussion of AI development races assumes that they have a definitive endpoint. Although some have hypothesized that if AI progress is discontinuous or sufficiently rapid then it could essentially have a definitive endpoint, the case for this remains speculative. It is therefore important to note that AI development may take the form of a perpetual R&D race: a race to stay technologically ahead of competitors rather than a race to reach some particular technological endpoint" (as indicated by Amanda Askell, Miles Brundage, and Gillian Hadfield in "The Role of Cooperation in Responsible AI Development").

Some experts denote the matter as the AI discontinuity hypothesis.

The usual viewpoint for the AI discontinuity hypothesis is that AI capabilities will somewhat erratically advance, such as large leaps followed by sizable lulls in advancement. Others assert that our advancement of AI will be more of a continuous process, gradually inching forward on advances in AI.

You've got the slow-and-sure camp versus the wild swings camp.

Conclusion

For the application of AI to the law, you can make use of either camp to try and predict the future of robo-lawyering and the like.

If you go with the slow-and-sure camp, the implications are that we will incrementally see AI being infused into LegalTech and ever so stepwise gradually move toward someday enabling autonomous AI legal reasoning systems. On the other hand, the wild swings camp would assert that we are bound to see long periods of no AI revelations in the field of law, punctuated surprisingly with sudden bursts of advancement.

Sorry to report that there is no meaningfully inarguable way to say that one camp is right and the other is wrong.

We should also consider how this discontinuity versus continuity impacts the efforts of applying the law to AI.

Based on the assumption that AI advancements will be continuous and gradual, we presumably will have sufficient time to craft new laws to cope with AI and ensure that we are regulating appropriately to deal with the *AI For Bad* aspects (such as AI that exhibits untoward biases and appalling inequities).

Meanwhile, if AI advancement is going to be discontinuous and nearly unpredictable, we will likely get caught off-guard from a legal angle. Laws that were already put in place about AI will suddenly be behind the times. Can we adjust those laws fast enough to contend with the abrupt and outsized AI advancements? Given the usual pace for drafting and passing laws to cover technological innovations, you would be prudent to have doubts about legal alignment arising on a timely basis.

There is little or no argument that we are all immersed in a high-stakes AI advancement or AI development race. This permeates all sectors and areas, including governmental entities, for-profit firms, nonprofits, and so on.

Believing though that the endpoint is solely the attainment of sentience is not useful and dreadfully misguides us all. There is a multitude of endpoints along the path of advancing AI. Whether we successfully achieve all those endpoints is unknown, let alone the sentience endpoint that is altogether hazy and not anywhere within eyesight.

A final comment for now.

We might be better off not even miraculously spurring AI sentience. For all we know, sentient AI might be like the proverbial bear in the woods. Humans could be facing down something that we aren't sure will decide to rip us to shreds.

I suppose the best thing to do in that case would be to have your running shoes ready and be prepared to run faster than your fellow humans if that's the kind of "humanitarian" approach you would prefer.

Note: *For supplemental materials depicting the aspects discussed in this chapter, refer to Appendix B, which contains various augmented diagrams, charts, and additional related facets of relevance.*

CHAPTER 13
AI & LAW:
AI WORST-CASE SCENARIOS

Key briefing points about this article:

- AI advancement is rapidly occurring and has generated intense interest all-told
- There is an increasing realization that AI can be used for dour purposes
- A poll of AI experts revealed six worst-case scenarios about today's AI
- These are realistic portrayals and not some kind of wide-eyed viewpoint
- We examine each of the worst-case scenarios from a legal and ethical AI mindset

Introduction

Recent polling of experts in the field of AI has identified six real-world AI worst-case scenarios that we are all going to face within our lifetimes.

Note that these scenarios are not of the sci-fi variety. In other words, you could easily do some wild conjuring and come up with plenty of AI nightmare scenarios. No doubt about it. The thing is, very few of those dystopian depictions would particularly be based on any semblance of reality.

We are not anywhere yet within the realm of the classic AI sentience takeover. You certainly know that trope of a dreadful tale. AI becomes sentient. Turns out the AI doesn't like us. Humans become enslaved to AI. If you want to make this even gloomier, AI wipes out humans entirely.

That was pretty easy to make up. Movies and TV shows produce that kind of hair-raising scary entertainment all the time. It would be nice though to sometimes be a bit more mindful of where AI technology is today and where it might reasonably be in the near future.

With that vital preface, let's go ahead and see what the polled AI experts came up with. Along the way, we will soberly consider the legal and ethical implications of each worst-case scenario. Please fasten your seatbelts for this AI imposing ride.

Dissecting Those Worst-Case Scenarios Of AI

We can briefly walk through each of the AI worst-case scenarios and explore their significance. I am listing them with a numbering indication, but this is not intended as a ranking or rating of the scenarios. The scenarios are all of the equal weight and the numbering is merely for ease of delineating them.

Scenario #1. Deepening DeepFakes Spurred By AI

This worst-case scenario entails AI being used to generate deepfakes.

You must already be vaguely familiar with deepfakes. The idea is that via the use of AI capabilities, it is increasingly feasible to create video, audio, and images that appear to be completely real but that are actually fakeries. One such example that recently went viral online showed what seemed to be Tom Cruise doing crazy antics, which though perhaps he's truly done so in the past, these latest videos were instead faked. The creator of the video used his own body in the videos and then utilized AI to superimpose Tom Cruise's face over his own face. It looks real.

In the past, those kinds of deepfakes weren't especially deep. They were relatively shallow. Anybody of even a modicum of sensibility could glance at the earlier spate of deepfakes and quickly point out that they were in fact fakes. Nowadays, it is much harder to so discern.

You can bet your bottom dollar that deepfakes are going to become nearly impossible to uncover their masquerade. The AI will do such a good job that there are no viable means of sorting the fakes from the real ones.

This might seem like a fun diversion, but the problem is going to be extraordinarily serious. Suppose a deepfake showcases a world leader announcing they are going to wage war with another country. Could the kneejerk reaction to this video prompt a war to occur? It could.

Besides the obvious ethical concerns, you can add legal considerations into the deepfake mix too. You are preparing a case for trial. You have a video that seems to exonerate your client. Unfortunately, the opposing side of the case claims that you are relying on a deepfake. It could be that you have no means to prove the validity of the video. Your case is sunk.

Scenario #2. AI-Based Autonomous Weapons Of Destruction

A popular movie from the 1960s consisted of a plot that involved a doomsday destruction machine that inadvertently gets triggered into action. The world comes to the brink of utter devastation in this award-winning and highly acclaimed classic.

This film was one of many at the time due to the cold war era and concerns that machines would act of their own accord by the hands of humankind that put those systems into motion.

Guess what, we are still in that same worrisome boat.

Indeed, the use of AI for the crafting of autonomous weapons is just getting started. There will be AI embedded into nearly all modern weaponry. Whether we will have any distinct control over those AI-powered weapons is a troubling concern.

Once again, the ethical qualms seem obvious. Destructive acts might happen so fast that there is no realistic way for humans to stop things before they go completely out of hand. Meanwhile, evildoers will readily relish those AI autonomous weapons, being able to wield great power without having to amass large armies of soldiers.

Some hope that we might legally establish international laws that will prevent the use of AI for autonomous weapons. You can set aside the unlikely hope of such a blanket outright ban. The odds are that the laws that might be enacted are going to be more so about mitigating the weaponry and require inspection and monitoring.

This Pandora's box is already partially open and cannot be shut closed.

Scenario #3. AI Further Erodes Our Privacy

The enormity of social media that spans the globe has led us to the realization that trying to retain a semblance of privacy is becoming harder and harder to do. AI is going to be an accelerant of privacy intrusion.

Here's a quick example you might not have thought of. AI-based self-driving cars are gradually going to become sufficiently capable to have them roaming our highways, byways, and neighborhoods streets. Those autonomous vehicles will be outfitted with a sensor suite consisting of video cameras, radar, LIDAR, ultrasonic units, thermal imaging devices, and the like.

I'm known for my ongoing exhortations that those sensor-laden autonomous vehicles will be capturing our daily lives via the use of those sensors, which I've coined as the *roving eye*. Wherever self-driving cars or trucks operate, they will be collecting data about whatever they perchance encounter on our streets.

Ethical and legal questions are just now starting to be floated. Who can access that collected sensory data? If it is stitched together, will it insidiously depict what we do and where we go, all day long and all night long? Do our existing laws provide sufficient protections regarding privacy concerns? Etc.

Scenario #4. Using AI To Occupy Our Attention And Sway Our Thoughts

Content that is tailored to you and your specific interests can be identified by AI capabilities and then shunted to your handheld smartphones. This seems glorious. Whereas you used to have to seek out content that was of interest to you, now the content comes right to you.

No need to lift a finger per se.

Ethical and legal qualms arise that the AI-infused content selectors are going to further divide us from each other as humans. Furthermore, the content can get us riled up. We also will potentially become preoccupied with the on-target content and lose our sense of self.

Could the AI manipulate us like rats in a Skinner box? I'm not suggesting the AI does this with an embodied sentience and only saying that the AI as devised by humans could work tirelessly and with human-led nefarious motives.

Scenario #5. AI Containing Untoward Biases And Promoting Inequities

Headlines keep pointing out that some of today's AI are built with inherent embedded racial biases, gender biases, and other inequity qualities. Sometimes this is due to an oversight by AI developers. Sometimes this is due to the nature of the AI tools being used. There are lots of ways this can arise.

Legal proposals are being considered for regulatory purposes to try and establish laws that will cope with these problematic AI aspects.

You can also assume that regardless of which new laws get enacted, there will still be legal actions even within prior laws that seek redress from those firms building and fielding such dour AI.

Scenario #6. Killing The AI Golden Goose Via Overstepped Laws

This last AI worst-case scenario turns the other scenarios somewhat on their heads.

In the other instances, the use of legal protections all seemed prudent and necessary. What might happen though is that the rush to create new laws about AI will end up curtailing AI innovations. The notion is that AI development gets crushed under the hefty weight of the legal sword.

The government might overregulate and essentially kill or at least maim the golden goose of AI.

Conclusion

You've now got six realistic worst-case scenarios about today's AI. There wasn't any flimflam about AI that goes berserk and takes over the world. We aren't at that stage, though we shouldn't rule it out as a further-term possibility as dependent upon breakthroughs in AI technologies and how humans cope with those advances.

Put on your legal cap and your ethics seeing glasses so that you can help in dealing with these six worst-case scenarios. The future is up to us all, and we have a chance at either preventing these AI worst-case situations or somewhat ameliorating them to be more judiciously handled.

Just to end on a somewhat eye-opening note, there are a lot more worst-case scenarios beyond these six. The counting has only just begun.

Note: *For supplemental materials depicting the aspects discussed in this chapter, refer to Appendix B, which contains various augmented diagrams, charts, and additional related facets of relevance.*

CHAPTER 14

AI & LAW: CHINA PROSECUTORIAL AI

Key briefing points about this essay:

- AI advancement is rapidly occurring and has generated intense interest all-told
- For those in the AI-in-the-law realm, AI is being increasingly used for legal tasks
- An AI system in China is reportedly been put in place to make prosecutorial decisions
- In particular, the decision of current focus is about whether to file charges or not
- We examine the nature of this AI and the tradeoffs in such legal usage

Section 1: Introduction

Prosecutors do a lot of legal tasks, of which a quite noticeable act entails deciding whether to file legal charges against someone.

There is oftentimes grayness in whether the filing of charges is warranted. Some prosecutors are considered more lenient than others in terms of when they choose to do a filling.

It has been voraciously claimed that there are prosecutors that are willing and eager to file charges at the mere drop of a hat. Others stubbornly refuse to file charges and it is said they require an extraordinarily heightened hurdle before they will opt to so proceed.

What goes into the decision-making process of a prosecutor that is faced with deciding to file charges or not do so?

You could point to seemingly tangible factors such as the nature of the crime and the presumed set of facts preliminarily collected. There is also the notion of the cost associated with pursuing the legal case and as weighed against the probability of attaining a conviction. On top of this is the perception of a track record of that prosecutor, such that the prosecutor likely wants to tout a high percentage of convictions and not be seen as failing to "win" in their pursued cases.

One supposes that you could readily add into the mix a fuzzy factor related to public awareness. Perhaps a prosecutor intends to send a message to the public at large, opting to make a big splash upon filing charges. This might be construed as a means of alerting society about whatever law enforcement philosophy the prosecutor wishes to widely convey. A skeptic or perhaps a cynic might also emphasize that the prosecutor could be making filing choices based on self-aggrandizement. The notion involves getting their name and claiming some fame from the filing decisions made.

All told, I believe we can reasonably agree that there could be a multitude of factors at play and that the filing of charges is bound to be a complex array of considerations. This type of decision would seem to defy any simplistic calculative method. Returning to the viewpoint of a skeptic or cynic, a snarky assertion would be that you could roll the dice as a random chance means of deciding to file charges, though I don't think society would accept that as a palatable method.

Why this extended discussion about the prosecutorial approach to filing charges?

Because a recent headline-grabbing pronouncement has boldly stated that China is now using an AI-based prosecutorial decision-making system to ascertain when to file legal charges. According to news reports, the AI is anointed to make these hefty decisions and do so somewhat autonomously, not having to first have a human double-checker review the choice or otherwise immerse a human into the process directly.

You might be tempted to construe that this implies AI has reached sentience. Nope. That would be a false conclusion. The system is the same kind of everyday nuts and bolts that go into the same AI that is being used to make mortgage loan decisions and render choices about which hair coloring selection is best for your head of hair.

It just so happens that China has opted to leverage that akin kind of algorithmic-based AI for the altogether serious and sober act of a prosecutor deciding to file legal charges.

Let's take a mindful moment to unpack the matter.

Digging Into The AI Prosecutorial Filing Charges System

According to the lead AI scientist that crafted the system, Professor Shi Yong of the Chinese Academy of Sciences, this latest capability is built upon a prior and still existent system known as System 206. System 206 was put into use by Chinese prosecutors in 2016. It was devised to aid human prosecutors by bringing together data and derived predictions regarding the strength of evidence for an arrest of a suspect, along with how dangerous the suspect is to the public at large, and also indicates the conditions of a suitable arrest.

The now more advanced system uses AI technologies to step into the role of decision-making about identifying and filing legal charges. A type of Natural Language Processing (NLP) feature is used to transform narratives regarding the circumstance into a machine-usable format. Reportedly, the use of Machine Learning is employed, a type of computational pattern matching.

An indicated 1,000 factors or variables are extracted from the transformed narratives and used to produce a filing decision.

The training data used to get the Machine Learning up-to-speed consisted of 17,000 cases that ranged from the years 2015 to 2020. Furthermore, not all types of crimes were selected. Instead, the training of this Machine Learning system was based on data from eight crimes, namely credit card fraud, obstructing official duties, theft, fraud, picking a quarrel, reckless driving, intentional injury, and running a gambling operation.

Why were only those eight crimes used?

Apparently, those are the eight most common crimes in Shanghai. The belief was that the first iteration of the AI ought to concentrate on crimes that are most frequently arising. This is a veritable "most bang for the buck" perspective. Once this AI seems to be working, a later iteration can add additional crimes to the base set.

This also brings up an associated and important point. The AI prosecutorial decision-making system is right now confined to being used at the Shanghai Pudong Procuratorate. Future expansion will require selecting crimes as relevant to other locales and obtaining needed data for pertinent training of the AI system from those locales.

One other notable claim made about the AI system is that it supposedly has shown a 97% accuracy rate at the filing of charges.

I would dare say that making such a bold declaration is both sloppy and improperly being touted. The 97% is seemingly based on the data used for training.

Allow me a moment to elaborate on this.

When training a Machine Learning system, you feed data into the computational pattern matching algorithm and mathematically patterns are sought. You typically hold back some portion of the data so that you can use it to test the pattern matching facility. The usual rule of thumb involves setting aside 20% of the data for testing and using the other 80% for the training.

Okay, so you do the training on the 80% and then proceed to feed the 20% into the pattern matcher to see if it can sufficiently make predictions across the test data. At that point, let's assume that 97% of the test data is aptly chosen for filing of charges as mated to the actuality of what occurred historically.

Does that somehow guarantee that for any other as-yet-seen data that a 97% accuracy is going to prevail?

Absolutely not.

The only statement you can assert is that for the training data collected, you attained a 97% accuracy on that set-aside test data. Beyond that, you are loosey-goosey about what might later on occur.

In the real world, the AI system might do dismally and be wrong a great deal of the time about choosing to file charges. There is a slew of concerns. Was the data from the 2015 to 2020 time period representative or somehow skewed? Is the data from the time period subsequent to 2020 on par with the historical data or have things changed? Etc.

Conclusion

Some have said that the beauty of using AI in this manner is that doing so will eliminate any bias on the part of human prosecutors that traditionally make the filing charges decisions. No more grandstanding by human prosecutors. The AI makes the choice, doing so without being steered or swayed by a human prosecutor that might have other motives in mind.

Sorry but that doesn't quite compute.

First, the data from the selected time period of 2015 to 2020 that was used for training Machine Learning was likely already imbued with preexisting biases. Suppose for example that during that time there were filing charges choices made that explicitly used racial, gender, or other inequity factors. The data reflects those biased choices. The odds are high that the computational pattern matching of the Machine Learning is going to inherit that same bias.

You might try to argue that perhaps there weren't any *explicit* biases by prosecutors during the 2015 to 2020 time period. On the other hand, suppose that there was *implicit* bias taking place. In that case, the data will again embody those biases and the odds are that Machine Learning will mathematically latch onto it.

In short, just because AI technology is being used, you cannot say for a certainty that bias has been eliminated. People seem to fall for the mental trap that due to the AI being a machine, the machine "must" be absent of any biases. Not so.

Another consideration is the nature of outliers. The Machine Learning approaches are usually attempting to mathematically find the most common tendencies. This means that outliers are often downplayed, ignored, or folded into the rest of the set.

I bring this up because you can imagine that if the AI opts to file charges on someone that raises the public ire, it could be that the AI did so inappropriately. If so, will human prosecutors countermand the AI or not? Likewise, suppose the AI declines to file charges on someone and this lack of a filing raises public ire. Will human prosecutors be able to nonetheless proceed to file charges?

I realize you could make the other side of that argument too. For example, the AI files charges, which raises public ire, and for which a human prosecutor might not want to take the heat so they drop the charges. This might be injustice in action. You could claim that the AI won't be subject to public pressures.

The same goes for the AI declining to file charges and yet the public insists that charges ought to be filed, for which a human prosecutor might acquiesce to such demands.

A final comment for now.

The public pressures are obviously going to vary in terms of significance as based on the overarching governance structure and culture of a society. In the case of China, using AI in this fashion is perhaps less daunting from a public perspective. You would not likely find such an easy acceptance in other venues, such as the United States.

You can expect that this kind of AI will be used in the U.S., though not given free rein. The notion of having an AI-based prosecutorial filing charges system as a handy guide for human prosecutors is abundantly feasible (well, some prosecutors would abhor it). Using such AI on an autonomous level is a far-future proposition, probably not even in our collective eyesight as yet.

Note: *For supplemental materials depicting the aspects discussed in this chapter, refer to Appendix B, which contains various augmented diagrams, charts, and additional related facets of relevance.*

CHAPTER 15

AI & LAW: GDPR XAI

Key briefing points about this essay:

- AI advancement is rapidly occurring and has generated intense interest all-told
- We are finding ourselves at the whim of AI-based decision-making algorithms
- It is reasonable to expect that the AI would explain its decisions (known as XAI)
- Efforts to craft AI-related regulations and legislation should include such provisions
- The GDPR provides legal language related to XAI and can be handily leveraged

Introduction

A significant concern about the advent of AI throughout society is the potential lack of explainability underlying how the AI works and makes various algorithmic decisions. In short, many of today's AI systems are opaque and contain seemingly inexplicable mathematical formulations, lacking a capacity to explain why a given decision was rendered.

We usually expect that we can get someone or something to explain why it is doing whatever it is doing.

Suppose you chat with a mortgage broker about seeking a new home loan. The broker asks you a series of questions about your financial situation, your job, and other facets of your personal circumstances. After collecting this altogether quite private information, the broker informs you that you do not qualify for a loan.

A decision has been made.

I'd bet that you would certainly ask why you've been turned down. In some locales, the law requires that you be told the basis for the turndown. The rest of the time it is a matter up to the broker to ascertain whether to explain the decision. Maybe the broker will do so, or maybe not. The broker might feel ethically swayed to provide an explanation. On the other hand, the broker might just decide that you are unqualified and not want to get any further into the details.

Let's revisit the scenario.

Instead of chatting with a human broker, let's go ahead and replace the human with an AI system that acts in the capacity of a mortgage broker. Once again, assume that you provide personal details and sadly get turned down for the loan.

Are you owed an explanation?

Akin to the situation with a human broker, some locales might require that an explanation be provided while other locales might not require it. If an explanation is not required, the AI might be programmed to provide an explanation anyway, or the AI might simply indicate that you've been turned down for the loan.

A convenient means of referring to AI that provides explanations is coined as XAI (explainable AI).

Some AI systems do not have any built-in features for generating explanations and therefore we would likely say that is lacking in any semblance of XAI. This could potentially be somewhat overcome by using an add-on tool that would interrogate the AI by using various technological methods and attempt to produce or reveal an explanation. Doing so is considered less robust than actually designing and building the AI from the ground up for being able to produce explanations.

All told, XAI can range from not having any XAI to embodying extensive XAI. Regrettably, you don't have any immediate means of knowing whether a given AI system has XAI or not. There isn't a rudimentary visual inspection that would showcase that XAI exists. Plus, perhaps surprisingly, the AI developers or others might claim that the AI does have XAI, though the proof would be in the pudding (i.e., check to see if an explanation is truly generated).

We can also add to the murkiness about XAI by pointing out that not all explanations are equally useful or equally valid. You see, I might hurriedly toss an XAI capability into my AI system and let it generate all kinds of wild and unsubstantiated explanations. Just because an explanation is produced does not necessarily suggest that the explanation is apt or even accurate.

XAI is gradually becoming a big topic of both legal and ethical AI concerns.

The EU anticipated these kinds of AI-based decision-making settings and opted to include in the General Data Protection Regulation (GDPR) an indication of fundamental rights related to the explainability of algorithmic decision making (ADM) systems. Note that AI is generally within the rubric of ADM (when the AI is used within the context of a decision-oriented task).

A key philosophical belief underpinning the GDPR is that individuals should be legally guaranteed transparency and should equally be guaranteed to not be subject to opaqueness when it comes to decisions impacting them.

A handy Technical Report (TR) by the European Commission Joint Research Center (JRC) indicates the core portions of the GDPR that relate to the explainability facets.

Let's unpack things and take a close look at those indications.

Digging Into Legal Stipulations About Explainability

We will explore seven core explainability precepts that have been conveniently noted in a *JRC Technical Report* co-authored by Ronan Hamon, Henrik Junklewitz, and Ignacio Sanchez and entitled "Robustness and Explainability of Artificial Intelligence."

As added clarification, the TR clearly states that the seven cited precepts are not the only ones within GDPR, so please be aware that there is more to this: "In addition to these rights, all the other ones generically referring to the processing of personal data also apply, namely the right of information (in a broader sense), the right of access, the right of rectification and the right to object, as well as the specific legal basis (art.6) used by the data controller (usually data subject consent)."

I'll describe each of the seven identified data protection rights that pertain to explainability and proffer a quick example to illustrate the nature of the right being depicted. As you'll see, I've numbered the indications, doing so merely for sake of discussion and ease of reference, which does not in any manner suggest a ranking or priority but only acts as an indexing convenience.

GDPR Selected Item #1: *"Right to be notified of solely automated decision making per Art. 13, Art. 14"*

This stipulation indicates that you are to be notified whether the decision-making process consists solely of an automated algorithm such as an AI system or whether a human is also involved.

You would certainly want to know.

I say this because suppose you assumed that only the AI was making the decision, and thus if you received an explanation from the AI it would seem to have encompassed all facets of the decision. But if a human was also secretly involved, you would likely want to find out what role the human additionally played and correspondingly obtain an explanation as to how the human entered into the decision that was rendered.

As an example, you apply for a mortgage loan and do so with what seems to be an AI conversational interactive system. You get turned down. You ask for an explanation. The AI perchance has an XAI capability. The AI explains the basis for the turndown. Unbeknownst to you, a human agent was tinkering in the AI or collaborating with the AI to make the decision. You had no means of knowing this. Furthermore, the AI explanation only presents the AI basis and does not explain the human influencer participation and their basis for the turndown.

By being made aware that the AI is not solely the decision-maker, you would be cognizant that any explanation ought to also include the additional human involvement too.

GDPR Selected Item #2: *"Right of notification and access to information about the logic involved in automated processing per Art. 13, Art. 14, Art. 15"*

This stipulation is relatively straightforward. You ought to be notified that an explanation can be made available. In addition, you ought to be notified regarding how to access the generated explanation.

In the example of the AI-based mortgage loan decision, if the system did not inform you that an explanation was going to be available, you'd have no idea that an explanation was able to be obtained. Of course, even if the system tells you an explanation can be made available, it must also indicate how to access it. An explanation that sneakily hides someplace does not do you much good.

GDPR Selected Item #3: *"Right on the information of the significance of and potential effects of solely automated decision making per Art. 13, Art. 14. Art. 15"*

This stipulation provides for a contextual indication around the nature of the AI as to what type of decision-making it is going to do and what impacts it might have upon whatever action you are undertaking with the AI.

Suppose you use an AI-based mortgage application system and do not realize that the AI per se will be the decision-maker. You might naturally think that the AI is only collecting data from you. Someone else or something else is going to make the loan decision, you would so assume. As such, the AI system should inform you beforehand about the extent of the decision-making (in the setting of a solely ADM).

GDPR Selected Item #4: *"Right not to be subject to solely automated decision making per Art. 22"*

This stipulation can give companies that are utilizing AI quite a hefty dose of heartburn. As indicated, those using the AI are presumed to be allowed to object to an AI-only decision-maker setting. The logical alternative is that you can either use a human decision-maker or use a combined AI and humans in the decision-making process.

Companies that are aiming to completely automate and use AI in the decision-making capacity are forced into having some alternative provision, which could undercut their efforts to reduce or entirely remove the human decision-making role. That makes automating the matter more complicated. Meanwhile, the rationale for individuals is that they ought to have an alternative to using just the AI, being able to invoke a human rather than being subject only to AI.

Let's consider that provision in our ongoing example. You are using an AI-based mortgage loan decision-making system. Perhaps you have qualms about how the AI is doing things.

You, therefore, request that the AI alone not make the decision. In whatever way the provider has set things up, they shunt you over to either a human agent or have the human agent work in conjunction with the AI on your loan application.

GDPR Selected Item #5: *"Right to contest a decision in solely automated decision making per Art. 22"*

This stipulation provides a means for the individual subject to the AI-only decision to contest the rendered decision.

You might argue that this is tangential to the explanation facets. It doesn't state that you are contesting the explanation, but instead contesting the decision (for which an explanation might or might not have been provided). In any case, it is an overall helpful stipulation.

Suppose you get turned down by the AI-only mortgage loan system. You contest the decision by signifying that you are contesting the AI result and want to have some recourse. This might get you shunted to a human agent. On the other hand, believe it or not, it could get you shunted to a different AI system that is used to override the other AI or at least serve in a contested assistance mode.

GDPR Selected Item #6: *"Right to obtain human intervention per Recital 71, Art. 22"*

This stipulation is a kind of *get me out of here* catchall. While in the midst of the AI decision-making, you request that a human intervene. Without this provision, you presumably could entirely be trapped within an AI-only scheme.

During your AI-based mortgage loan interaction, you get frustrated and request that a human intervene. A human agent then comes into the mix. Note that this does not necessarily require the human to undertake the decision. The AI can presumably still be used. The bottom line is that you have a human now also intermixed into the matter.

GDPR Selected Item #7: *"Right to obtain an explanation per Recital 71"*

This stipulation is the on-target as it is a *no-bones about it* assertion that an explanation is to be provided if you wish to get one. Notice though that the provision does not require that the explanation be forced upon you. You need to ask for it, thus the subtle but telling wording that you have a right to obtain it.

You use the AI-based mortgage loan system and it turns you down. No explanation is necessarily provided. You though opt to request one, for which the system is supposed to comply and provide an explanation.

Conclusion

There are some qualms that the explanation-oriented provisions can be tripped up by clever AI developers that wish to subvert the intent of the GDPR provisions. As you might have noticed when discussing the stipulations, there are problematic ways to try and seemingly be compliant with the rules and yet still somewhat skirt them.

The devil is in the details, as they say.

The good news is that at least such XAI-related rules are included in the GDPR. There are many other regulations in other countries that do not have any similar set of provisions, or that have provisions of an even weaker nature. For those that are trying to craft AI-related legislation and regulations, it would be useful to take a closer look at the explainability aspects and make sure that as much as possible there are relatively ironclad provisions included.

I'd dare say that such sound advice doesn't seem to need much more of an explanation, for now.

Note: *For supplemental materials depicting the aspects discussed in this chapter, refer to Appendix B, which contains various augmented diagrams, charts, and additional related facets of relevance.*

CHAPTER 16

AI & LAW: DATA POISONING

Key briefing points about this essay:

- AI is increasingly being used throughout societal applications
- This is partially attributed to the advent of Machine Learning and Deep Learning
- These AI techniques tend to require lots of data for training purposes
- Someone nefarious can attempt to add foul data to confound the AI
- Coined as data poisoning, we examine the legal and ethical AI impacts

Introduction

Let's talk about data poisoning.

The topic is a rising societal concern and will continue to loom over our heads due to the expanding advent of AI and especially the frequent use of Machine Learning (ML) and Deep Learning (DL).

All told, the notion is that someone might surreptitiously "poison" the data that goes into an AI system and ergo try to trigger the AI into doing something untoward or perhaps prod the AI into acting in a dire and reprehensible manner.

Let's start with a brief backgrounder about ML/DL in general.

Machine Learning and Deep Learning consist of a form of computational pattern matching that relies extensively or entirely on data. The notion is that data is fed into an ML/DL algorithm for training purposes. Mathematical patterns are presumably discovered in the data and this becomes the means for the computer to then, later on, do akin pattern detection in freshly presented data.

Consider for example the use of ML/DL for facial recognition.

We might feed into a given ML/DL algorithm a set of pictures containing the faces of people. The ML/DL identifies patterns in the data such as the facial features of a nose, eyes, mouth, ears, and so on. The training data has to be mindfully provided since otherwise the ML/DL would not be able to find suitable patterns for trying to identify faces (suppose all the faces were covered up or blurry, this would make the pattern matching establishment problematic).

Henceforth, when given a picture and seeking to ascertain whether a person's face is shown in the snapshot, the ML/DL scans the photo for the expected features. If the features are sufficiently shown, the image is indicated as containing a face, else the ML/DL would report that a face does not seem to be in the picture.

So far, so good.

Imagine that we are developing a self-driving car and want to ensure that Stop signs are readily identified while the autonomous vehicle is roaming the streets. We could collect together a bunch of pictures containing Stop signs and feed that as data into an ML/DL. The AI algorithm would presumably discover patterns such as a Stop sign is red in color, it is a particular shape, it has the word "Stop" in it, etc.

We then associate within the AI driving system that whenever a Stop sign is detected that the AI will bring the car to a safe halt. This seems quite straightforward.

Let's do something evil and see if AI can be tricked. Suppose that when the ML/DL is being trained, we put into the data a whole bunch of photos of signs that say "Slow" and are yellow in color. The ML/DL now has two different kinds of signs being fed into the training process. A human would realize that these are two completely different types of signs. The ML/DL has no such common sense or any innate capacity to "comprehend" this difference.

As such, the ML/DL would likely discover two sets of patterns for the act of stopping, one that consists of a red sign with the word "Stop" and another consisting of a yellow sign with the word "Slow" on it. If both of those conditions are associated with bringing the autonomous vehicle to a halt, we are going to have a problem on our hands. Just envision a human driver that is driving behind a self-driving car that keeps suddenly and wrongly coming to a halt whenever a Slow sign is seen.

You could say that we poisoned the data that was being used to train the AI.

This poisoning can occur when the ML/DL is first trained during the AI development process. In addition, the poisoning can occur after the initial training, namely being fed in "live" while the AI system is relearning on the fly or adjusting itself over time (the AI is considered in production or being actively put into use).

A quick example consists of detecting email that is spam.

Most of the existing major email systems use AI-like capabilities to try and discern whether an email is spam or not. You've likely noticed that oftentimes your email system will place emails into a spam folder for you, having somehow opted to mark the email as being spam.

How did the email system figure out that the email was spam?

One method consists of logging the number of times that people signified that the given email was spam. If there are a lot of people indicating that the email is spam, this is a likely indicator that it probably is spam. You end up benefiting from the wisdom of the crowd, whereby oodles of other people perchance took the time to mark the email as spam, and therefore the email system can catch the particular email when it comes to you and place the email into your spam folder.

Those that are creating spam emails do not want their email to be tossed into the spam folder.

They want to somehow confound the spam detection and ensure that their email offering a fortune or other get-rich schemes will land in your regular email box. Those con artists don't likely have a ready means of altering the email system per se, such as wanting to change the programs underlying the email system, and must instead find a sneakier *outsider* means of confounding the email system as it stands.

Here's what they could do.

They rig up a slew of fake email boxes that will report to the email system, just as though they were ordinary email boxes of everyday people. They send the spam email to those rigged email boxes. They then have the rigged email boxes mark the spam as not being spam. If they can do this to a high enough volume, the number of reported "not spams" will overshadow the number of reported spams.

Thus, the email system will simply now presume that the alleged spam email is not spam, and will henceforth let the email go straight through into your email box.

Do you see how this illustrates the aspect of data poisoning?

The email scammers are feeding poisoned data into a real-time AI-like system. The AI merely accepts this data and adjusts accordingly. No one is the wiser.

A handy report by the European Commission concerning various emerging AI issues describes data poisoning this way: "It consists in deliberately introducing false data at the training stage of the model. This can be done to neutralize a system, reduce its performance, or silently introduce a backdoor exploitable by the adversary. Data poisoning relies on the capacity of models to learn new patterns along the time by constant retraining almost in real-time using newly acquired data. This design opens the possibility for an attacker to inject gradually benign data that will progressively drift away from the decision boundaries of the algorithm. Similarly, reinforcement learning systems can easily be misled to maximize wrong goals by corrupting the reward channels of their agents" (as per the JRC Technical Report on "Robustness and Explainability of Artificial Intelligence" by Ronan Hamon, Henrik Junklewitz, and Ignacio Sanchez).

There are sensible ways to set up an AI system to try and defeat these data poisoning efforts.

First, the AI developers need to be cognizant of adversarial attacks that might be launched against their AI system. If the AI developers aren't thinking about such possibilities, the odds are that they are leaving all sorts of open-ended paths for data poisoning. Cyber hackers and other bad hat actors are bound to figure out a means to carry out malicious ways to poison and inject the foul data.

Second, numerous cyber security precautions should be put in place. Preparations need to be made to prevent (at least) both availability attacks and integrity attacks. In an availability data poisoning attack, the attacker overwhelms the AI by flooding foul data into the ML/DL, clogging it up and likely bringing the AI system overall to a halt until things are righted. For an integrity-style data poisoning attack, the integrity is comprised of feeding judicious amounts of foul data, such as the earlier examples of the spam email and the Stop sign.

Third, per the use of cybersecurity methodologies such as the Department of Defense (DoD) and its Cyber Maturity Model Certification (CMMC), the AI system should be carefully protected and kept secure.

The four rudimentary principles entail securing the network connecting to the AI, the physical facility hosting the AI, the endpoints that feed data into the AI, and the people that have access to the AI system in any developmental or similar capacity.

Now that we've covered the core precepts underlying data poisoning, we can jump into the legal and ethical concerns about this burgeoning weakness of today's AI.

AI In The Law And The Specter Of Data Poisoning

Let's discuss some key principles of AI-in-the-law and then we'll be ready to tackle the legal and ethical considerations of data poisoning.

Please be aware that there are two major ways to intertwine AI and the law: (1) AI as applied to the law and the practice of law, (2) Law as applied to the advent of AI.

In the first instance, lawyers and legal scholars emphasize the use of AI as applied to the law, which I'll signify as the so-called robo-lawyer, robo-judge, robo-juror, and the like kinds of aspirations. Note that I am not a fan of that robo verbiage, but it is admittedly a quick way to invoke the imagery of what applied AI is ultimately aiming to do.

The second instance consists of applying the law to AI, such as ascertaining how our laws and regulations should be adjusted or crafted anew to cope with the burgeoning use of AI throughout society. This is construed as using legal acumen to figure out the appropriate means of governing AI.

Much of the flashy aspects about AI-in-the-law stems from the application of AI into the law (that's the first case indicated above).

Especially popular ways of applying AI in the law consist of infusing Natural Language Processing (NLP) capabilities into the arduous chore of doing e-Discovery (i.e., AI-based NLP is especially useful when dealing with large-scale narrative-oriented datasets that require extensive and otherwise laborious by-hand legal discovery efforts). And you are perhaps familiar with the use of AI for aiding in examining and composing legal contracts. There are lots of these infusions taking place of plopping AI techniques and technologies into the carrying out bona fide legal tasks.

Get ready for the next boon, namely the need to apply the law to AI. This is gradually gaining notable ground and outstretched headlines. Why so? This is partially due to the rampant and uncontrolled promulgating of AI that has showcased seedy and untoward capacities. The recent era of AI began with a rousing cheer that AI would be abundantly good for society, but quickly discovered that there is the grimy underbelly of AI too. AI systems are now suspect right away, often embedding contemptible biases in factors such as race, gender, etc. As a result, the application of the law to AI is garnering a lot of steam.

With those two sides of the coin on the table, we can take a closer look at data poisoning.

If an AI system gets undermined by data poisoning, the result could be harmful to those that are either directly reliant upon the AI or that are indirectly reliant in some secondary fashion. The harm could range from a mild form of harm such as merely being inconvenienced or could reach dour heights that might entail physical harm or even death.

Who is to be held responsible for AI that is perturbed by data poisoning?

The typical naive answer is that AI is the responsible party. The AI is somehow assumed to embody a semblance of human agency. We don't have that kind of AI these days. We do not have sentient AI. We don't know if AI sentience is even possible.

Claims that the AI has acted of its own will are relatively disingenuous at this time (though, it is hard to predict what the future might hold, which of course the aspirational goal of AI researchers is to someday attain sentient AI).

The gist is that there are humans that set up the AI and put it into use. Legally, we presumably would seek redress from those that established the AI or are maintaining or otherwise fostering the AI.

Lawyers versed in the legal machinations associated with AI systems will increasingly be sought for legal cases entailing AI that goes off the rails, either by its internal auspices or by external cyber-attacks. In addition, there are many efforts underway to draft and enact laws specifically targeting the AI realm. Lawyers are needed to aid in the creation and passage of such laws and/or will be needed once such laws are put onto the books.

Conclusion

The other side of the AI-in-the-law coin requires that we also consider how data poisoning could impact AI-infused LegalTech.

You decide to make use of an AI-based billing system for your legal practice. Unbeknownst to you, there is a means for a data poisoning action that can confound your billings and seemingly reduce or erase the billings for a particular client. That's bad.

A court adopts an AI-powered system that indicates sentencing recommendations. Turns out that via a data poisoning attack, the AI is confounded to recommend lowered sentences. A convicted criminal might have hired a bad hat actor to use such an attack in advance of their sentencing.

The point overall is that AI systems applied to the law are equally exposed to data poisoning vulnerabilities.

Those that are developing and fielding AI should be abiding by ethical AI guidelines and astutely ensuring that their ML/DL is not so readily data poisoned. Existing laws and the proposed AI regulations that are being pursued will add a legal hammer to the proper ethical practices.

The antidote for data poisoning requires due diligence, legal savviness, and ethical AI entailment.

Note: *For supplemental materials depicting the aspects discussed in this chapter, refer to Appendix B, which contains various augmented diagrams, charts, and additional related facets of relevance.*

CHAPTER 17

AI & LAW: ADVERSARIAL ATTACKS

Key briefing points about this essay:

- AI is increasingly being used throughout societal applications
- This is partially attributed to the advent of Machine Learning and Deep Learning
- A cybersecurity ploy to undercut the AI consists of adversarial example attacks
- Someone nefarious can attempt to confound or inappropriately trigger the AI
- We examine the legal and ethical AI impacts

Introduction

There is both a sense of fun and also seriousness that can be found when examining optical illusions.

You might be familiar with a famous optical illusion that was first devised by psychologist Edgar Rubin in 1915 that is still floating around today and frequently pops up online and delightfully so appears abundantly in social media postings. The iconic image is generally known as Rubin's Vase or alternatively coined as Rubin's Faces.

This rather simple and legendary image consists of a center portion that appears to be a rough outline of a vase. But if you slightly alter your gaze, you might also see what appears to be two faces, whereby there is a face to the left of the vase that is turned toward the vase and a second face on the other side of the vase that is likewise facing the vase. In short, you might visually interpret the image as though it is merely two people facing each other and there is a small gap between their faces.

Does that ring a bell as to the image that I am referring to?

If not, you might want to take a quick look online and do a search for the iconic optical illusion.

The reason that I draw your attention to optical illusions is due to an attempt to explain how a quite unsavory and dangerous method of cyberattack is brewing related to AI. The method is commonly referred to as an adversarial exemplar attack. This ostensibly clever form of attack can confound an AI system that is reliant upon Machine Learning (ML) and Deep Learning (DL) techniques.

Generally, it is possible to get an AI system to make a wrong move or take an untoward action via the adversarial exemplar attack, depending upon the exploitable weaknesses of the fielded AI.

The topic is a rising societal concern and will continue to loom over our heads due to the expanding advent of AI and especially the frequent use of Machine Learning and Deep Learning. All told, the notion is that someone might feed specially seeded data into an AI system and ergo try to trigger the AI into doing something untoward or perhaps prod the AI into acting in a dire and reprehensible manner.

The beauty of this attack, if we are willing to call it beauteous, entails the fact that the foully seeded data is not readily detectable by human eyes and otherwise appears to be completely harmless and resembles entirely the normally suitable data being fed into the AI system. That makes this an especially tough nut to crack. Humans would not be the wiser. The data looks seemingly normal. Hidden within is a triggering element of data that the ML/DL will detect and get triggered into potentially dreadful action.

You might say that this is akin to a type of optical illusion. Humans see one thing, the AI sees something else. It is an insidious notion and one that will increasingly be deployed by bad hat actors and other such evildoers.

To further explain how this works, let's start with a brief backgrounder about ML/DL in general.

Machine Learning and Deep Learning consist of a form of computational pattern matching that relies extensively or entirely on data. The notion is that data is fed into an ML/DL algorithm for training purposes. Mathematical patterns are presumably discovered in the data and this becomes the means for the computer to then, later on, do akin pattern detection in freshly presented data.

Consider for example the use of ML/DL for facial recognition.

We might feed into a given ML/DL algorithm a set of pictures containing the faces of people. The ML/DL identifies patterns in the data such as the facial features of a nose, eyes, mouth, ears, and so on. The training data has to be mindfully provided since otherwise the ML/DL would not be able to find suitable patterns for trying to identify faces (suppose all the faces were covered up or blurry, this would make the pattern matching establishment problematic).

Henceforth, when given a picture and seeking to ascertain whether a person's face is shown in the snapshot, the ML/DL scans the photo for the expected features. If the features are sufficiently shown, the image is indicated as containing a face, else the ML/DL would report that a face does not seem to be in the picture.

So far, so good.

Imagine that we are developing a self-driving car and want to ensure that Stop signs are readily identified while the autonomous vehicle is roaming the streets. We could collect together a bunch of pictures containing Stop signs and feed that as data into an ML/DL. The AI algorithm would presumably discover patterns such as a Stop sign is red in color, it is a particular shape, it has the word "Stop" in it, etc. We then associate within the AI driving system that whenever a Stop sign is detected that the AI will bring the car to a safe halt. This seems quite straightforward.

Suppose further that when the ML/DL was being trained that it was also separately fed data about posted signs that said Go. These signs would have the word "Go" on them, be green in color, have a different shape than Stop signs, and for all apparent purposes be completely unlike a Stop sign. The ML/DL gets trained on these Go signs and the action associated with the AI driving controls is to keep the autonomous vehicle going ahead whenever such a sign is detected.

In recap, the ML/DL is computationally able to pattern match on Stop signs and also on Go signs.

Humans can easily do the same. If you show a human driver a Stop sign, they will presumably and immediately tell you that it is a Stop sign, thus a driven vehicle should be brought to a stop. If you show a human driver a Go sign, they will presumably and immediately tell you it is a Go sign and ergo an indication to proceed.

The ML/DL now has two different kinds of signs that were fed into the training process. A human would realize that these are two completely different types of signs. The ML/DL has no such common sense or any innate capacity to "comprehend" this difference.

Here's what an evildoer might figure out.

The mathematical means of the ML/DL doing the computational pattern matching might entail analyzing the images of Stop signs and Go signs at a pixel level. I'm sure you know that pixels are those tiny dots that compose a picture. You can zoom into the details of an image and look at the thousands of pixels that make up the image.

It is conceivable that by manipulating an image at the pixel level, we could take an image of a Stop sign and adjust it to appear to be a Go sign in some significant respects. This could potentially be done in such a manner that when glancing at the image overall, it still looks like a Stop sign. But when digging deeper into the pixels, the image seems to be representative of a Go sign.

Humans would usually look at such a picture on an overarching basis and see just a Stop sign. The ML/DL would be examining the pixels and reach a conclusion that the sign is a Go sign. I realize this seems nearly unimaginable that one such sign could be so differently interpreted. In a manner of speaking, you could suggest that it is an optical illusion, similar to Rubin's Vase. How you look at the image will seem to tell a different story.

A handy report by the European Commission concerning various emerging AI issues describes adversarial exemplar attacks this way: "The most active research domain currently is, without doubt, the domain of adversarial examples. It consists in using input data to the trained machine learning model, which is deliberately designed to be misclassified. The development of techniques to this end has been an active area of research, with a host of different types of attacks, relying mostly on optimization procedures to synthesize adversarial examples. Most of the attacks focused on classification tasks in computer vision, this subdomain being one of the most active areas of deep learning research. Deep learning image analysis systems have been proved to be sensitive to input image spoofing of various kinds" (as per the JRC Technical Report on "Robustness and Explainability of Artificial Intelligence" by Ronan Hamon, Henrik Junklewitz, and Ignacio Sanchez).

In case you are thinking that this form of attack could only occur related to visual imagery, there are other ways this kind of nefarious attack can be undertaken.

One notable example involves language translation. We nowadays are fortunate to have computing that will readily translate from one natural language to another. If you are traveling in Germany and are an English-speaking tourist, you can conveniently use your smartphone to aid in doing translations for you.

Researchers showcased a type of attack whereby they were trying to take advantage of a weakness or flaw in a popular online language translating AI-based system. They fed this sentence in English into the AI translating system: "People sitting in a dim restaurant eating." The correct translation is this: "Leute, die in einem dim Restaurant essen sitzen." That is indeed what the translation system produced.

Note that the German word "essen" is indicative of the English word of "eating" (this is going to be important in a moment herein).

The researchers then fed this English sentence: "People sitting in a living room eating." For all general impressions, this sentence seems quite similar to the first sentence, namely that people are sitting around and eating. The only difference seems to be the location of the eating activity. We would not though presumably construe that as especially bothersome when doing a translation.

Turns out that the sentence was translated into: "Leute, die in einem Wohnzimmeressen sitzen." The English equivalent would be that people are sitting in a living room. Nothing about the act of eating is expressed in this translation.

The researchers had figured out that a weakness or flaw existed in the online AI translating tool. By intentionally shaping an input phrasing, they could get the weakness or flaw to be invoked. The developers of the translation tool might be utterly unaware that the flaw exists.

As such, an evildoer that is aware of the flaw could potentially exploit the matter at will. For further background on such attacks, see the ICLR 2018 conference paper entitled "Generating Natural Adversarial Examples" by Zhengli Zhao, Dheeru Dua, and Sameer Singh.

There are sensible ways to set up an AI system to try and either not include such flaws or attempt to detect when data being fed into the ML/DL is seeking to trigger an inappropriate action in this sneaky means. I'm sure you've deduced by now that the reason this is known as an adversarial exemplar attack is that it is a cybersecurity-related approach of an adversarial nature that uses selected or devised "examples" of data to get an AI system to be triggered in some attacker desired means.

The attacker does not need to alter the programming or coding of the AI system. Instead, they simply "trick" the AI to act as it has already been programmed to do, though presumably not acting in the contextual way that the AI developers originally envisioned.

As an aside, there is an ongoing argument being made as to whether this is fairly described as a flaw. Some developers would insist that it isn't a flaw. It is merely a *feature* and one that can either be invoked with good intentions or be invoked with bad intentions.

This brings us to the legal and ethical AI aspects of this topic.

AI In The Law And Adversarial Exemplar Attacks

Let's discuss some key principles of AI-in-the-law and then we'll be ready to tackle the legal and ethical considerations underlying adversarial exemplar attacks.

Please be aware that there are two major ways to intertwine AI and the law: (1) AI as applied to the law and the practice of law, (2) Law as applied to the advent of AI.

In the first instance, lawyers and legal scholars emphasize the use of AI as applied to the law, which I'll signify as the so-called robo-lawyer, robo-judge, robo-juror, and the like kinds of aspirations. Note that I am not a fan of that robo verbiage, but it is admittedly a quick way to invoke the imagery of what applied AI is ultimately aiming to do.

The second instance consists of applying the law to AI, such as ascertaining how our laws and regulations should be adjusted or crafted anew to cope with the burgeoning use of AI throughout society. This is construed as using legal acumen to figure out the appropriate means of governing AI.

Much of the flashy aspects about AI-in-the-law stems from the application of AI into the law (that's the first case indicated above). Especially popular ways of applying AI in the law consist of infusing Natural Language Processing (NLP) capabilities into the arduous chore of doing e-Discovery (i.e., AI-based NLP is especially useful when dealing with large-scale narrative-oriented datasets that require extensive and otherwise laborious by-hand legal discovery efforts). And you are perhaps familiar with the use of AI for aiding in examining and composing legal contracts. There are lots of these infusions taking place of plopping AI techniques and technologies into the carrying out bona fide legal tasks.

Get ready for the next boon, namely the need to apply the law to AI. This is gradually gaining notable ground and outstretched headlines. Why so? This is partially due to the rampant and uncontrolled promulgating of AI that has showcased seedy and untoward capacities. The recent era of AI began with a rousing cheer that AI would be abundantly good for society, but quickly discovered that there is the grimy underbelly of AI too. AI systems are now suspect right away, often embedding contemptible biases in factors such as race, gender, etc. As a result, the application of the law to AI is garnering a lot of steam.

With those two sides of the coin on the table, we can take a closer look at adversarial exemplar attacks.

If an AI system gets undermined by an adversarial exemplar attack, the result could be harmful to those that are either directly reliant upon the AI or that are indirectly reliant in some secondary fashion. The harm could range from a mild form of harm such as merely being inconvenienced or could reach dour heights that might entail physical harm or even death (imagine a Stop sign rigged to secretly portray a Go sign, for which an AI-based self-driving car might be fooled into proceeding ahead when it should not be doing so).

Who is to be held responsible for AI that is perturbed by this trickery?

The typical naive answer is that AI is the responsible party. The AI is somehow assumed to embody a semblance of human agency. We don't have that kind of AI these days. We do not have sentient AI. We don't know if AI sentience is even possible. Claims that the AI has acted of its own will are relatively disingenuous at this time (though, it is hard to predict what the future might hold, which of course the aspirational goal of AI researchers is to someday attain sentient AI).

The gist is that there are humans that set up the AI and put it into use. Legally, we presumably would seek redress from those that established the AI or are maintaining or otherwise fostering the AI.

Lawyers versed in the legal machinations associated with AI systems will increasingly be sought for legal cases entailing AI that goes off the rails, either by its internal auspices or by external cyber-attacks. In addition, there are many efforts underway to draft and enact laws specifically targeting the AI realm. Lawyers are needed to aid in the creation and passage of such laws and/or will be needed once such laws are put onto the books.

Conclusion

The other side of the AI-in-the-law coin requires that we also consider how adversarial exemplar attacks could impact AI-infused LegalTech.

You decide to make use of an AI-based billing system for your legal practice. Unbeknownst to you, there is a means for triggering the AI via an adversarial exemplar attack that can confound your billings and seemingly reduce or erase the billings for a particular client. That's bad.

A court adopts an AI-powered system that indicates sentencing recommendations. Turns out that via an adversarial exemplar attack, the AI is confounded to recommend lowered sentences. A convicted criminal might have hired a bad hat actor to use such an attack in advance of their sentencing.

The point overall is that AI systems applied to the law are equally exposed to adversarial exemplar attacks.

Those that are developing and fielding AI should be abiding by ethical AI guidelines and astutely ensuring that their ML/DL is not so readily tricked. Existing laws and the proposed AI regulations that are being pursued will add a legal hammer to the proper ethical practices.

The antidote for coping with adversarial exemplar attacks requires due diligence, legal savviness, and ethical AI entailment.

Note: *For supplemental materials depicting the aspects discussed in this chapter, refer to Appendix B, which contains various augmented diagrams, charts, and additional related facets of relevance.*

CHAPTER 18

AI & LAW: RESPONSIBLE AI

Key briefing points about this essay:

- AI is increasingly being used throughout societal applications
- Unfortunately, a lot of AI is getting devised that entails *AI For Bad*
- Such AI exhibits racial biases, gender biases, and other inequities
- One means to cope entails pairing attorneys with AI developers
- The gap between them needs to be lessened, aiming to have AI-savvy lawyers

Introduction

A recent research article posits an intriguing legal-oriented saga that reveals the innate value of having AI-savvy lawyers that can impart their legal acumen in a technologically realistic way.

Or, conversely, showcases the difficulties and challenges that can arise when legal talent being utilized is bereft of adequate understanding about what today's AI can accomplish.

Are you ready for a quick rundown of the telling tale?

I'll paraphrase in my own manner of writing style.

Assume that a company proffering a social media platform is seeking to deal with societal qualms that the postings on the site ought to not be of an inciting nature. Trying to use human labor to scrub the enormous social media site is not particularly feasible due to the vast volume of postings and the rapid pace at which postings arise.

Thus, a more prudent notion involves using automation to detect the inciting material and correspondingly remove it from the site. To this specific task, an AI system is devised. The AI developers do their darnedest to leverage the latest in AI techniques and technologies, including Machine Learning (ML) and Deep Learning (DL), hoping to have the AI excise any and all inciting content.

After much arduous effort, the AI team proudly displays that the programmed AI is able to remove about 90% of the posted inciting material. Pop those bottles of champagne.

The AI though also ends up removing some content that is non-inciting, doing so inadvertently as part of the process of seeking out the inciting content. Of the presumed inciting content, turns out about 20% is actually non-inciting. You could say that this represents a semblance of false positives, whereby the AI falsely marked as inciting some content that by subsequent human inspection was ascertained to be non-inciting.

The legal counsel of the firm is dismayed by the capability of the devised AI. What kind of AI is this that removes so much of the non-inciting content? Go back to the drawing boards. So, the team leader of the AI development effort seeking clarity asks the legal counsel whether a reduction in the amount of non-inciting content would suffice. Counsel replies affirmatively.

Working late nights and weekends, the AI team tweaks the AI system and tries earnestly to resolve the non-inciting overstep. They are proud once again to now demonstrate that the AI only removes about 5% of the non-inciting content. Applause is warranted.

A bit of a less cheery aspect is that now the success rate of detecting and removing inciting content has dropped down to 70%. In short, the non-inciting removal has been relatively curtailed, yet doing so at the cost of rather dramatically lessening the catching of inciting material.

Woe is me, the social media company might say.

How are we do analyze the situation and learn some valuable lessons?

Per the researchers: "Following several frustrating rounds, new insights have emerged: the legal counsel has learned the inherent precision-recall trade-off. In addition, the team leader realized that the definition of inciting content that was used in the process of labeling the training data was too simplistic. The legal counsel could have helped clarify the complexities of this concept in alignment with the law. The team leader and the counsel regretted not working together on the project from day one. As it turns out, both were using the same words, but apparently, much of what they meant has been lost in translation" (as indicated in the *Communications of the ACM*, February 2022, "Data Science Meets Law" by Shlomi Hod, Karni Chagal-Feferkorn, Niva Elkin-Koren, and Avigdor Gal).

You might assert that at times there is a knowledge gap between those developing AI systems and the legal beagles that are brought into such matters for their legal insights.

As suggested by this example, it could be that lawyers are sometimes unfamiliar with how AI systems work and can have outsized expectations accordingly. There are plenty of additional issues to be dealt with. AI development efforts frequently tend to seek out legal opinions long after the concrete has already been poured and become solidified, so to speak.

Last-minute actions of suddenly asking for a legal blessing of an AI system are bound to be bad for everyone involved. All kinds of rework might be needed, which could have been better undertaken at the start of the endeavor.

AI In The Law And The Making Of Responsible AI

Applying the law to AI is gradually gaining notable ground and outstretched headlines.

Why so?

This is partially due to the rampant and uncontrolled promulgating of AI that has showcased seedy and untoward capacities. The recent era of AI began with a rousing cheer that AI would be abundantly good for society, but quickly discovered that there is the grimy underbelly of AI too. AI systems are now suspect right away, often embedding contemptible biases in factors such as race, gender, etc. As a result, the application of the law to AI is garnering a lot of steam.

Who is to be held responsible for AI that is perturbed by this trickery?

The typical naive answer is that AI is the responsible party. The AI is somehow assumed to embody a semblance of human agency. We don't have that kind of AI these days. We do not have sentient AI. We don't know if AI sentience is even possible. Claims that the AI has acted of its own will are relatively disingenuous at this time (though, it is hard to predict what the future might hold, which of course the aspirational goal of AI researchers is to someday attain sentient AI).

The gist is that there are humans that set up the AI and put it into use.

Legally, we presumably would seek redress from those that established the AI or are maintaining or otherwise fostering the AI.

Lawyers versed in the legal machinations associated with AI systems will increasingly be sought for legal cases entailing AI that goes off the rails, either by its internal auspices or by external cyber-attacks. In addition, there are many efforts underway to draft and enact laws specifically targeting the AI realm. Lawyers are needed to aid in the creation and passage of such laws and/or will be needed once such laws are put onto the books.

We must close the gap between those that develop AI and the legal teams that can aid in giving suitable legal guidance along the way.

In a similar fashion, the researchers describe the situation this way: "The growing prevalence of AI systems, as well as their growing impact on every aspect of our daily life create a great need to that AI systems are 'responsible' and incorporate important social values such as fairness, accountability and privacy. It is our belief that to increase the likelihood that AI systems are 'responsible,' an effective multidisciplinary dialogue between data scientists and lawyers is needed. Firstly, it will assist in clearly determining what it means for an AI system to be responsible. Moreover, it would help both disciplines to spot relevant technical, ethical and legal issues and to jointly reach better outcomes early in the design stage of the system" (per the article by Hod, Chagal-Feferkorn, Elkin-Koren, and Gal).

They say it takes two to tango, which in the case of devising sound AI systems, you would be wise to ensure a proper and timely pairing of AI developers and pertinent attorneys. I say pertinent due to the added caveat that it would be best to include AI-savvy attorneys, if at all feasible. Otherwise, the legal prowess being included is potentially going to inadvertently steer an AI effort sideways, not realizing what AI can and cannot today do.

Conclusion

The researchers cited herein are trying to aid in conquering that divide between technologists and attorneys by having put together an innovative class on Responsible AI. Fully titled as a course in *Responsible AI, Law, Ethics, and Society*, a decidedly multidisciplinary approach is taken to the class. Those wanting to be primarily technologists are included, as are those that are pursuing a legal career. Joint teams are required when solving assignments. Various real-world AI tough problems are assigned, encompassing the realms of discrimination and equality, liability and responsibility, privacy, and transparency.

This is a quite laudable effort.

One bit of a gotcha for anyone wading into the Responsible AI arena is the muddy and murky waters of ascertaining exactly what responsible AI denotes. An open question is postulated by the researchers: "There is no crystallized consensus of what 'Responsible AI' consists of and how it should be taught. We had to develop our own working framework for this course, a framework that must be dynamically adapted based on evolving research and practices. On a similar note, student evaluation is another key issue: What does it mean to be competent in Responsible AI?" (per Hod, Chagal-Feferkorn, Elkin-Koren, and Gal).

Despite these vagaries, these kinds of innovative course offerings are sorely needed and tremendously welcomed. In fact, any bona fide attempts of nearly any kind at increasing awareness about the need for and advent of Responsible AI is a worthwhile pursuit.

Lawyers are needed in the quest for Responsible AI. Even better still are lawyers that are up-to-speed about AI, sufficiently so that they grasp the real versus the fakery about AI.

A long and treacherous path is ahead for the burgeoning use of AI throughout society, and whether many know it or not, attorneys are going to be greatly needed during this perilous journey. Yes, we'll be inexorably thankful that legal minds are engaged.

Note: *For supplemental materials depicting the aspects discussed in this chapter, refer to Appendix B, which contains various augmented diagrams, charts, and additional related facets of relevance.*

CHAPTER 19

AI & LAW: MAP OF PATH AHEAD

Key briefing points about this essay:

- AI in the law is gaining speed and increasingly being applied to many legal uses
- Usual ways of applying AI include e-Discovery, doing legal contracts analyses, etc.
- Some lawyers are behind the times and either ignoring the advent of AI in the law or believe it irrelevant to them
- The ABA has passed a resolution associated with the importance of attorneys being cognizant of AI aspects
- To some degree, you could argue that knowing about AI and the impacts thereof are a duty of being an attorney

Introduction

Let's discuss Artificial Intelligence (AI).

Most lawyers have undoubtedly heard about or even directly experienced the use of AI-infused apps in their everyday lives.

The use of facial recognition to unlock your smartphone and the soon-to-be IRS-required facial recognition to access your personal tax records is technologically made feasible due to AI capabilities, like it or not.

When you speak to Alexa or say hello to your Google conversational device, you are making use of AI-based Natural Language Processing (NLP) that translates your spoken words and attempts to affably interact with you.

In brief, AI is here to stay and will steadily continue to advance. It will become embedded into all manner of systems and devices. There will be no viable means of escaping the ubiquity that AI capabilities will power amongst the myriad of daily services and goods that we all consume.

Shifting focus, consider how AI is entering into the legal domain.

Perhaps somewhat surprisingly, those deeply immersed in the legal field are oftentimes only vaguely aware of how AI is inexorably getting intertwined within the practice of law and the future of law itself. This is easy to understand as AI has only been scratching at the edges of the legal realm and just inching its way in.

Furthermore, an oft-stated axiom about the legal arena is that it seems to be one of the last sectors or industries to generally embrace technology all told. Tried and true methods of using paper-based approaches or staying the course with faxes are seemingly hard to give up. Suspicions about using new technology are at times perhaps justified per overly steep learning curves or due to earnest qualms about cybersecurity vulnerabilities, yet meanwhile advancing tech typically referred to as LegalTech continues to inexorably gain traction and is being intricately woven into the underlying fabric of modern-day legal offices.

Where there is LegalTech, there will eventually also be AI.

That seemingly brazen precept is altogether straightforward. Whatever type of legal aiding piece of automation you might envision or seek to obtain will ultimately have AI included. Doing so will boost ease of use, proffering cognitive-like sensibilities, and make legal work more productive and efficient (assuming the AI is judiciously included and equally wisely utilized by the legal teams). At times, the AI will be somewhat awkwardly bolted onto a legal tool that otherwise has already been in existence and needs to after-the-fact bolster its functionality. In other instances, the AI will be built into a legal tool from the ground up, serving as the cornerstone for the resultant legal app.

But before we get ahead of ourselves regarding this look at AI in the law, we need to ensure that the big picture is on display.

To do this, put your mind toward the idea of a two-sided coin.

The Two-Sided Coin Of AI In The Law

Please be aware that there are two major ways to intertwine AI and the law: (1) AI as applied to the law and the practice of law, (2) Law as applied to the advent of AI. You might say that they are two sides of the same coin.

In the first instance, lawyers and legal scholars emphasize the use of AI as applied to the law, which I'll signify as the so-called robo-lawyer, robo-judge, robo-juror, and the like kinds of aspirations. Note that I am not a fan of that robo verbiage, but it is admittedly a quick way to invoke the imagery of what applied AI is ultimately aiming to do.

The second instance consists of applying the law to AI, such as ascertaining how our laws and regulations should be adjusted or crafted anew to cope with the burgeoning use of AI throughout society. This is construed as using legal acumen to figure out the appropriate means of governing AI.

Much of the flashy aspects about AI-in-the-law stems from the application of AI into the law (that's the first case indicated above). Especially popular ways of applying AI in the law consist of infusing Natural Language Processing (NLP) capabilities into the arduous chore of doing e-Discovery (i.e., AI-based NLP is especially useful when dealing with large-scale narrative-oriented datasets that require extensive and otherwise laborious by-hand legal discovery efforts). And you are perhaps familiar with the use of AI for aiding in examining and composing legal contracts. There are lots of these infusions taking place of plopping AI techniques and technologies into the carrying out of conventional legal tasks.

The use of AI as added onto or embedded into LegalTech is the most commonly noticed facet of AI in the law.

Get ready though for the next boon, namely the need to apply the law to AI.

This is gradually gaining notable ground and outstretched headlines.

Why so?

This is partially due to the rampant and uncontrolled promulgating of AI that has showcased seedy and untoward capacities. The recent era of AI began with a rousing cheer that AI would be abundantly good for society, but quickly discovered that there is the grimy underbelly of AI too. AI systems are now suspect right away, often embedding contemptible biases in factors such as race, gender, etc.

As a result, the application of the law to AI is garnering a lot of steam.

Lawyers are needed that understand the in's and out's of AI. What weaknesses of AI are exploitable by evildoers and garner legal exposures accordingly? How can laws be crafted to stymy the *AI For Bad* emergence? Will such laws be crafted to keep AI innovation steaming ahead or will new regulations undercut the advantages of AI?

You see, some rightfully worry that the wrong kind of laws, though perhaps created with the most earnest of intentions, will ostensibly kill the golden goose.

Generally, AI-infused systems have the upside of potentially being better at what they do and are more societally beneficial than ordinary tech, but they also spur the chances of violating the four key principles of embodying what is handily abbreviated as *FACT*, namely that AI ensures fairness, accountability, transparency, and ethical conduct in its computational actions.

There are many efforts underway to draft and enact laws specifically targeting the AI realm, occurring at the federal level and the states level (plus internationally too). Lawyers are needed to aid in the creation and passage of such laws, plus will later be needed once such laws are put onto the books to help interpret and adjust those laws.

Consider another important avenue that will require attorneys with legal-oriented AI-savviness.

Who is to be held responsible for AI that goes astray and performs untoward actions?

The typically knee-jerk answer is that AI is the responsible party. The AI is somehow assumed to embody a semblance of human agency. We don't have that kind of AI these days. We do not have sentient AI. We don't know if AI sentience is even possible. Claims that the AI has acted of its own will are relatively disingenuous at this time (though, it is hard to predict what the future might hold, which of course the aspirational goal of AI researchers is to someday attain sentient AI).

The gist is that there are humans that set up the AI and put it into use.

Legally, we presumably would seek redress from those that established the AI or are maintaining or otherwise fostering the AI. Companies that have crafted AI systems will need lawyers that know how to internally guide the AI building efforts to minimize AI-arising legal problems down the road. Firms that have already put forth AI apps are likely to find themselves facing legal wranglings when the AI they've released fails to abide by the fairness and allied precepts.

Lawyers will inarguably be needed by those companies as they fend off legal challenges.

Meanwhile, individuals that believe they have been wronged by the AI are apt to seek legal representation and legal advice about how to proceed with a legal case against those AI-producing or AI-using firms. The overarching notion is that lawyers versed in the legal machinations associated with AI systems will increasingly be sought for legal cases entailing AI that goes off the rails.

Conclusion

A final remark, for now, might spur added mindfulness for you about the heightening significance of AI in the law.

Some would vigorously argue that lawyers are professionally obligated to know about AI in the law by the very canons of legal conduct as required by the *ABA Model of Rules*, particularly pertaining to the venerated Duty of Competence. A somewhat admittedly under-the-radar resolution of the ABA declared this rule: "RESOLVED, That the American Bar Association urges courts and lawyers to address the emerging ethical and legal issues related to the usage of artificial intelligence ("AI") in the practice of law including: (1) bias, explainability, and transparency of automated decisions made by AI; (2) ethical and beneficial usage of AI; and (3) controls and oversight of AI and the vendors that provide AI" (per American Bar Association, House of Delegates).

This provides extra fodder for the assertion that attorneys ought to be immersing themselves to some reasonable degree into the AI-in-the-law realm.

Notice that I said that legal professionals can aim to be *reasonably* versed.

One false objection by some is that getting into the AI topic requires a nerd-like grandiose high-tech background or perhaps entails doing arcane computer programming akin to a super techies skillset. Not so. Though digging deeply into the tech might be desired by some lawyers, there is no such necessity for those that want to be less entrenched but yet also still be able to sufficiently partake in the AI-in-the-law facets (not everyone has to be a lawyers-that-code adoptee).

You can go the route of aiding the inclusion of AI into legal tools and LegalTech systems, bolstering those efforts by the keenness of your legal prowess. That's the side of the coin entailing AI as applied to the law. A smattering of AI familiarity would typically suffice. Your profound knowledge of the law and the practice of law provide the sorely needed domain knowledge for such efforts.

Or you can participate in the crafting of new laws that will provide added safety and equity for the pell-mell rush of AI throughout our society. Once again, familiarity with AI will be sufficient, while your ample legal acumen is the overriding criterion.

Besides the regulatory perspective, you could perhaps be ready to serve your existing clients as they find themselves confronting AI-related systems exposures or calamities. You might even consider establishing a new line of your legal practice that will aid businesses and individuals that find themselves wronged by AI systems. These are all lawyering activities that fit into the side of the coin of applying the law to AI.

I trust that this provides a kind of helpful map to you, illuminating the path ahead that AI in the law will be indomitably forging.

There is no need to arbitrarily flip a coin to try and guess whether AI in the law is going to be substantial. Of the various bets that you might wish to make as a lawyer, betting that AI is coming and will inevitably permeate the legal field is a guaranteed winner. It is, shall we dare say, a sure bet?

Note: *For supplemental materials depicting the aspects discussed in this chapter, refer to Appendix B, which contains various augmented diagrams, charts, and additional related facets of relevance.*

CHAPTER 20
AI & LAW: ROBO-JUDGES XAI

Key briefing points about this essay:

- AI is increasingly being used throughout societal applications
- In the legal field, there is an ongoing exploration of having AI robo-judges
- There are a slew of tradeoffs about whether to use AI robo-judges or not
- One concern is that seemingly robo-judges won't have sufficient explainability
- There are nuances to this contention that need to be put on the table

Section 1: Introduction

We've got a lot to cover.

Let's dive immediately and without hesitation into a repeated assertion that explainable AI (known commonly as XAI) is said to be a knockout showstopper when it comes to formulating AI-based robo-judges.

I will stridently argue herein that this is an inadvertently misleading assertion. It seems to be compounded at times via a kind of echo chamber amongst some in this realm that generally seems to accept the claimed contention as true at face value.

A handy unpacking would seem advantageous to all parties.

First, some quick background to make sure we are on the same page.

Explainable AI is a subfield within the overarching realm of AI. The notion is that any AI system that especially entails some form of algorithmic decision-making (ADM) ought to be able to explain how it reaches whatever decision was being computationally tackled. This indubitably makes sense that we would want AI to provide an explanation that underlies the "reasoning" for any computational decisions being made.

We certainly expect that humans will explain their reasoning for notable decisions. If you go to a medical doctor and the physician prescribes some special medicine and recommends extended bedrest, you would rightfully seek to get a cogent explanation for the prescribed medical advice. Of course, some medical doctors might gruffly refuse to provide an explanation, or might insist that you won't understand it, but in the end, the odds are that the physician would have to proffer some basis for making the medical decision.

This example of the medical doctor showcases that explanations are particularly valued when a decision is within a significant context. If you ask a child whether they want chocolate ice cream or vanilla ice cream for dessert, and the child responds gleefully that they want chocolate ice cream, there is probably not a compelling reason to have the child explain their reasoning. You can certainly encourage the child to think about how they arrived at the decision, though there isn't any life-or-death or similar heftiness on the line that suggests an explanation must be elicited.

Another salient feature of the medical doctor example is that an explanation can vary dramatically as to the nature of the explanation per se. Imagine that the medical doctor utters arcane medical terminology to you while explaining the rationale for the medical decision made. Such an explanation might do the receiver of the explanation little good. We also have to consider that an explanation is not necessarily apt. The medical doctor might explain that it was a sunny day and that's why the medicine and bed rest was recommended. This seems quite out of sorts and not related to the decision context.

There are a plethora of additional nuances associated with explanations, which I've covered elsewhere in greater detail, but herein this brief glimpse will suffice for now.

In the medical doctor saga, replace the human medical doctor with an online AI medical-oriented system. Envision that you entered your symptoms into the AI and it produced the recommendation about getting medicine and extensive bed rest. Would you want the AI to be able to explain how it arrived at this medical advice? Sure, nearly anyone would.

Another arena in which the stakes are high enough that we would normally expect an explanation entails the role of human judges.

When a trial judge makes a decision during a court case, we would likely expect that the judge would explain the basis for the decision. This transparency is part and parcel of our existent viewpoints about the rule of law. Judges ought to not be making decisions that are somehow random or arbitrary. Instead, we expect that judges will make sound decisions that are amply backed by an explanation or logical rationale.

Keep in mind that a judge might provide an explanation in the same manner as to the varieties and vagaries found within the medical doctor example. The judge might provide a pointedly short shrift explanation. The explanation might be couched in arcane legal language. The explanation might or might not seem sensible. And so on. Akin to a box of chocolates, you do not have an ironclad guarantee that the explanation will be cleanly sound and full-bodied.

A handy balancing mechanism in the case of a judge is that the decision and its explanation (or lack thereof) can be later called into question. There is a means of pursuing legal redress for what might be argued as a faulty decision by a judge. In that sense, the explanation provided by the judge can be quite crucial for trying to ascertain the legal merits and strength of the legal decision rendered.

All told, it is quite reasonable to say that we fully expect judges to proffer explanations underlying their judicial decisions. Not all such explanations are equal, namely, some explanations are terse, some are weak, some are strong, some are overblown, some are off-target, etc.

We are now ready to start discussing AI-based judges.

I am loath to refer to AI in a legal judging capacity to be coined as a robo-judge. There are numerous pitfalls in using the robo-judge moniker.

One qualm is that it brings forth imagery of a walking-talking robot that will sit in a courtroom akin to where a human judge would reside. We presumably might someday have such robots, but for now, the plainer version is an AI system of the modern-day ilk like any other AI system of today's flavor. When you speak to Alexa or Siri, it is not a robot in the fashion of humanoid-like machinery. It is just a speaker with a microphone. In that same frame of reference, an AI judge could be less obtrusive-looking than a walking-talking robot.

By stating that an AI judge is a robo-judge, there is a knee-jerk reaction to assume that the AI must be a walking-talking robot. This in turn causes a raising of the eyebrows as to whether the robo-judge notion is farfetched and a sci-fi oddity. Let's put aside that kind of imagery and simply agree that an AI system in a legal judging capacity could be of a wide range of machinations and appearances.

Admittedly, it is easiest to bring up the AI-based legal judge topic by mentioning the robo-judge vernacular. The utterance gets attention and brings the listener or reader into the matter with an almost instantaneous form of recognition.

I have already invoked the robo-judge moniker herein, and will for convenience of discussion continue to do so further throughout this discussion. Meanwhile, set aside the sci-fi imagery and instead focus on the AI software rather than the hardware embodiment.

We've not set the stage for jumping into the explainable AI and robo-judge controversy.

Explainable AI And The Robo-Judge

We can start by almost overwhelmingly concurring that an AI-based robo-judge must have an explanatory facility, such that it in some manner entails an explainable AI capacity (i.e., that it has XAI). I don't think anyone would sensibly disagree with that assertion.

That being said, there have been some that suggest we might eventually drop the need for XAI in the matter of robo-judges, doing so under the apparent and inevitable belief that we might always accept the AI legal judging rulings and no longer question why or how the AI reached a judicial decision. I am skeptical that humans subjected to an AI legal judge would give up the explanatory requirement, so I put this argument about someday willingly tossing aside the XAI of a robo-judge as not especially viable in the foreseeable future.

Another angle is that perhaps in the dire rush to put in place AI robo-judges, we are willing to shunt to the side any needed XAI. We'll let the XAI catch up later on. The logic is that the beneficial aspects of the robo-judge outweigh the perceived requirement of having XAI. For the time being, it seems we might begrudgingly settle on the value provided by robo-judges and hesitatingly accept the omission of XAI.

Though that might seem persuasive, serious doubts arise that an AI robo-judge in any bona fide legal context would be construed as acceptable when it lacked XAI. You might try to argue that if the robo-judge is deciding parking tickets, this doesn't need any XAI.

The counterargument is that you likely would still insist on XAI, even if it was rather sparse and simplistic, such as merely indicating that because you parked illegally as per the facts of the case, you are guilty of the parking infraction.

Recall that we have already acknowledged that explanations can range widely in terms of depth and substance. The parking ticket robo-judge would seemingly still need to have XAI, though the XAI is straightforward and readily generated.

All in all, let's then stick with the viewpoint that XAI of a robo-judge is an incontrovertible requirement.

Since we of a reasonable nature are all in agreement on this, the case seems to be closed. Just make sure an AI robo-judge has XAI and we are done with this discussion. No further debate ensues.

The twist is that trying to include XAI into a robo-judge is currently somewhat vexing.

Here's the usual reason why this is so (some added background will be first indicated).

Much of the current focus on AI consists of using Machine Learning (ML).

You can think of Machine Learning as a form of computational pattern matching. Typically, you feed training data into an ML algorithm and an attempt is mathematically made to find patterns by the computer-based program. After having landed hopefully on identifiable patterns, you can place the AI ML into use. Any new data fed into the ML will become subject to the pattern matching and the AI system can indicate whether the pattern is found or not found (or, using probabilities, indicate a likelihood of being found or not being found).

There are various statistics-like Machine Learning algorithms that can be utilized.

In addition, another variant consists of what is commonly denoted as Deep Learning (DL). The usual approach for Deep Learning entails setting up an Artificial Neural Network (ANN), which resembles superficially the notion of neurons and neural networks of the human brain (a computational version, almost like a simulation, though much inferior to true neural networks). To be clear, ANNs are not anywhere close to the nature and magnificence of human wetware, as yet, and therefore be extremely cautious in currently overstating what these artificially concocted computational pattern matching machinations can achieve.

The problem becomes that when using some of these Machine Learning and especially Deep Learning approaches, there are no easy means to generate an explanation. The convoluted nature of the computations and the intricate mathematical formulations do not lend themselves to being depicted as a crisp set of logical narratives that we would expect of an everyday explanation.

In a simplistic but hopefully revealing anecdotal indication, imagine if you asked why the medical doctor recommended that you be given special medicine and extended bed rest, and the explanation was that this decision was based on adding together the values of 2, 10, 28, and 35, which in total led to 75. And that 75 somehow means to recommend the medicine and the bedrest.

You would undoubtedly be scratching your head and the explanation is ostensibly of no notable value to you.

The crux then of the lack of XAI for AI robo-judges is that if we are sticking with the existing formulation of AI as based on today's semblance of Machine Learning and Deep Learning, there is a decidedly aching problem that we cannot surface narrative style logic-based explanations of the ilk that we expect to have.

A robo-judge that recounts the explanation that the decision to not allow a crucial piece of evidence at trial is due to the values of 2, 10, 28, and 35, which totals to 75, and thusly makes a judicial ruling that the evidence shall not be admitted, well, this is not a viably useful explanation.

We are now at the precipice of the problem at hand.

XAI has been argued herein as a requirement for robo-judges, which most of us would reasonably agree is a requirement. But the use of AI that consists of ML and DL is currently generally bereft of narrative-style logic-focused explanations. Thus, if we have XAI and it only spits out numeric values, this is not in any sensible fashion a proper form of explanation. We would construe this as essentially having no XAI at all.

Our impeccably logical conclusion is that since we must have XAI for the robo-judges, but the prevailing approach to AI using ML/DL seems unable to acceptably produce XAI capacities, this obviously means that we must delay the advent of robo-judges. You could extend this logic and say that the delay will be possibly a long time in duration, perhaps even forever, under the cornerstone assumption that the XAI will never be feasible in these conditions.

Therefore, cross off robo-judges from your list of things to do, since without XAI they are dead in the water. XAI is the showstopper. Even if other as yet settled AI aspects are required for establishing robo-judges, we have found either the weakest link of them all or certainly at least one keystone weak link.

Sorry, robo-judges, it sadly seems that your time is not now and might not ever arrive.

Counterarguments About Attaining XAI

Let's take a swing at some counterarguments on this seemingly gloomy conclusion about XAI and robo-judges.

First, we do not know that the Machine Learning of today will prevail as the Machine Learning of tomorrow. This is a twofold consideration.

There is a chance that the AI techniques and technologies underlying ML will improve and we will indeed find ways to generate plausible and logically sensible explanations out of the underlying computational morass. Anyone tossing in the towel that there is zero chance of deriving useful XAI from ML is standing out on a ledge. Already there are promising approaches starting to emerge. You can expect that this will continue as a forceful interest by AI researchers and AI developers for years to come.

In addition, as a second related consideration, we do not even know that the formulations of ML and DL as we construct them today are what the future of ML/DL consists of. There could readily be some other approaches that gradually emerge. And within those approaches might be a more suitable way to tie in XAI.

Secondly, there is a tendency these days to have rejected out of hand any other form of AI other than the use of ML/DL. The prior era of symbolic-oriented AI has been placed on the junk heap by some. We do not know that this absolute rejection is sensible.

In short, we might combine the symbolic approach with what some refer to as the ML/DL subsymbolic approach. This is commonly referred to as a hybrid symbolic-subsymbolic combination. In that case, we might rely upon the symbolic portion for the generating of the XAI, while allowing the subsymbolic to be either not explained or explained via some higher-level explanatory logic that we overlay onto the subsymbolic structures and computational algorithms.

The gist of these counterarguments is that anyone tossing in the towel about XAI for robo-judges is doing so prematurely. They are either unaware of the preceding considerations or are aiming at a point in time that they are not explicitly stating when the robo-judges might be crafted. If you are explicitly stating that robo-judges put into place tomorrow are insufficient due to XAI as a bottleneck, perhaps you might be on some reasoned ground.

But this takes us to the third and quite altogether important angle on this matter.

The third major counterargument involves the subtle though the entirely vital realization that we cannot say with any certainty how humans generate explanations, and ergo we have potential latitude about how we might get AI to generate explanations. This might seem a bit mysterious or mystifying, so we need to dig into it.

Can you tell me how a human being generates an explanation?

The correct answer is that you cannot do so, not at least to the degree of shall we say wetware neural circuitry in the brain that produces an explanation. There is no means as yet to reverse engineer the neural network of the human mind such that we can trace how an explanation is logically and internally generated within our noggins. You might be able to say that this neuron or that neuron fires or activates, but this is not viably tied to the logical explanation that we expect humans to provide.

If you asked the medical doctor or a judge to explain how they generate explanations, I dare say that none of them would indicate that first this neuron did this, and then this other neuron did that, and so on. They would instead provide a (hopefully) cogent indication that they pieced together this part of a narrative and this part of a narrative, which ultimately forms the logical expression of their explanation.

They are pretty much clueless as to how their brain actually undertook this. You can further suggest that they are providing an explanation based on what they've been taught about explanations or that they learned over time from childhood about what an explanation consists of. Whether this is innately wired into the brain or a learned facet is still open to debate.

If you are now generally convinced that we do not yet know how the brain produces an explanation, you have stepped into the XAI topic in a manner that you might not have realized.

For those that decry that Machine Learning or Deep Learning is potentially mathematically and computationally inscrutable and thus it defies the generating of an explanation, how then do you explain the fact that humans generate explanations and yet they seemingly do not know how their brains do so?

The key point is that if humans are seemingly concocting explanations based on the matter at hand, we could presumably do likewise with AI that is based on current day ML/DL. Without even waiting to see what advances in ML/DL might come down the pike, we can overlay an explanation facility on top of the ML/DL and rely upon this as the XAI generator.

A retort is that this is a second-hand explanation, rather than presumably first-hand as to natively derived by the ML/DL itself. But you would seemingly acknowledge that the explanation generated by a human is seemingly second-hand and not first-hand, namely that a human contrives an explanation.

We can go a step further and emphasize that at least in the case of an XAI that serves in this second-hand role, it is likelier more transparent than the opaqueness of the human mind. We don't especially have any direct means of examining the human mind explanation generator. We have a direct means of doing so for any sensibly coded XAI.

Conclusion

Before we leap to the conclusion that XAI is the holdback of robo-judges, we need to realize that the XAI of today is being confounded so far by the methods of ML/DL that we are using today. Future methods of ML/DL might differ, such that XAI is more readily feasible. In addition, the hybrid symbolic-subsymbolic might lend itself to an easier entry into XAI capabilities.

We also should be cautious in rejecting an XAI-overlay approach, since you could argue that humans are already using an overlay approach to apparently how they generate explanations.

I am not equating the human mind to the AI of today, so please realize that those two should not be compared side by side. The notion is simply that the overlay XAI is worthy of apt attention in these matters.

Finally, there are a lot of other AI-related aspects that will feed into the building and fielding of AI-based robo-judges. Many of those AI aspects are also still being figured out or will not be discovered or invented for a while to come (well, we hope they will in fact be discovered or invented). This gives the XAI some breathing room to get figured out. You would be somewhat hard-pressed to allege that the XAI issues of today are alone holding back the robo-judges of today.

This also is a reminder that there are shall we say thin or lite versions of robo-judges and thick or heavy versions of robo-judges. For the thin or lite versions, a modicum of XAI might be sufficient, even if it is rather simplistic or brittle. You have to be careful about lumping all robo-judges into the same pot, and likewise be mindful of not lumping all XAI facilities into the same barrel either.

Broad and all-encompassing claims that XAI is the showstopper or knockout of achieving AI-based robo-judges seem a bit overstretched and should be revisited. As they say, we just need to make sure that we know our limitations.

Note: *For supplemental materials depicting the aspects discussed in this chapter, refer to Appendix B, which contains various augmented diagrams, charts, and additional related facets of relevance.*

CHAPTER 21
AI & LAW:
AI AS BOARD MEMBER

Key briefing points about this essay:

- AI is increasingly being used throughout societal applications
- Suppose that AI becomes advanced enough to serve in human-like roles
- In particular, envision AI becoming a board member of a corporation
- We can postulate about the legal ramifications of this radical notion
- It is quite unlikely in the near term but worthy of legal exploration anyway

Introduction

I'd like to bounce a seemingly wild idea off you, which I hope won't cause you to roll your eyes and react as though the idea is utterly preposterous.

Are you ready?

Suppose we included AI into a corporate board of directors.

Now, this might seem relatively tame, namely that the possibility of a board of directors opting to use AI would be ostensibly sensible and not at all untoward. For example, a board might have a special corporate portal that provides vital metrics and reports about the status of the firm. And within the portal, we might provide an AI-based analysis tool that would search for interesting patterns within the company data and showcase those patterns to board members.

That all seems straightforward.

But, shift your attention to a more puzzling angle of the use of AI in the context of a corporate board. Let's say that we put an AI system into the board as a bona fide and legally engaged member of the board. The common way to express this is that we would have a robot serving as a board member of a corporation. This board-seated robot would have the same duties, responsibilities, and all the same legal entanglements as would a human board member.

Does that make your head spin?

It might.

One of the reasons that I don't like to refer to such a board seat as being occupied by a robot is that it conjures up the sci-fi imagery of a Terminator-like robot that walks and talks. Maybe another similar variant would be a Robocop of the same-named movie fame. We rightfully get goosebumps at the notion of such a robot.

Furthermore, we don't have robots yet of that kind of sci-fi variety. Sure, some robots can kind of walk and talk, you've likely seen these on social media postings. Those robots though are extremely crude and are not at all fluid or fluent in how they function. Someday we are inevitably going to witness the more humanoid resembling robots, but we aren't there yet.

To thusly discuss a board seat being occupied by a "robot" is immediately rejected by many that find the concept ridiculous, unrealistic, and pure fancy. I would ask that you put aside the robot imagery and instead focus on the AI aspects. Envision that we had an AI system that perchance was capable of performing board duties. The AI itself might not necessarily be a robot per se. When you chat with Alexa or Siri, you do so via your smartphone or a speaker resembling a device. Think of that kind of machinery as the interface for AI.

If you are willing to entertain the seemingly outlandish possibility of AI being a board member, we can next dig into some of the legal details that arise accordingly. For those of you that believe we will never experience AI in a board seat capacity, you might nonetheless still find the discussion about AI as a board member to be somewhat intriguing even if odd.

AI In The Law That Deals With Corporate Boards

Researchers are seriously and soberly examining the legal implications of AI board members.

One noteworthy consideration is whether AI board members would be acting in and have liability akin to their side-by-side human board members: "For example, if the appointment of a voting robot as a director on a corporate board becomes the norm in industry practice, such a change gives rise to questions as to the status of such a robot director in relation to its human counterparts and the status of its vote. These questions would be of a policy nature; for example, choosing to regard robot directors on par with human directors would give rise to issues such as how legal personality and liability should be structured, and choosing not to consider robot directors on par with human directors would give rise to questions of attribution of agency and liability instead" (as indicated in the *Berkeley Business Law Journal*, "Technology vs Ideology: How Far Will Artificial Intelligence and Distributed Ledger Technology Transform Corporate Governance and Business?" by Iris Chiu and Ernest Lim).

A subtle point in that noted question is the relevant idea that these AI board members would somehow need to be appointed to a board. We wouldn't expect that AI would magically appear on a board of directors. Instead, in the same manner, that humans get appointed to boards, the AI would presumably need to likewise get so anointed to such a position.

Why in the world would shareholders of a company opt to vote for including AI as a board member?

You can, surprisingly perhaps, identify numerous sensible reasons for doing so. Whereas a human board member might change their tune once they get onto a board, shareholders might believe that an AI board member would be more consistent. An AI board member might also be less emotionally reactive when making heavy board decisions. Shareholders might also have greater transparency about the board activities due to being able to readily have the AI indicate what it is doing and why it is making board decisions in the manner so being undertaken.

There are though plenty of downsides about an AI board member. The AI could certainly "change its mind" while serving on a board, though I want to emphasize that the AI that we know of today does not have a mind in the meaning of human minds. Consider simply that the AI programming changes, either by human hand or by the AI modifying itself, ergo you could suggest this was a changing of viewpoints regarding board matters by the AI.

We also cannot assume that the AI would be necessarily transparent. It could be that the AI is based on complex computational intricacies that are mathematically sound and yet there are no viable means of turning that into a logically understandable narrative. There is also the aspect that the AI might be locked down and no one can peer into the programming and data that the AI has been set up with.

I appreciate that you are staying with me on this demonstrably wild ride. There's more.

Suppose that the AI board member renders a "bad" decision that causes corporate harm in one manner or another: "In this scenario, will personal or product liability arise where a poor directorial decision is made that results in a corporate loss? Petrin posits that only product liability is relevant, as there is no further relevance for personal liability If shareholders appoint AI to be the management organ, shareholders would not sue themselves for being negligent principals. Möslein also posits that, where the ex-post accountability of an AI director is irrelevant, as there is no capacity to account nor compensate, AI directors have to be ex-ante programmed to discharge directors' duties. However, he questions how such duties can be 'internalized' by machine learning. Can we really fuse the requirements of corporate law into product liability law? In this respect, a number of commentators have opined that a regulatory agency that sets ex-ante governance standards may be optimal, particularly with respect to software standards and entailing the liability of software providers" (as per Chiu and Lim).

Lots of additionally vexing facets arise. We might reasonably be worried that a cyberattack at the AI board member might undercut the AI and it falters or fails to perform its intended duties. An equally worrisome scenario involves a secret cyber breach that rewires or recodes the AI to do the bidding of the bad hat actor. Having AI be in the rarefied air of serving on a board could be seen as dicey. Board members can wield great power and shape the strategy and direction of a firm.

If you noodle on the AI board member notion, you might find other intriguing avenues of potential distortions or concerns. Suppose that the human board members are suspicious of the AI or want to sway the AI to the side of the human board members. The human board members could try some tricky end around to get the AI to see things their way.

As the researchers keenly mention, where there is a will there is a way: "Because AI is designed by humans for humans, AI is likely to mirror and entrench the views of humans. Management could influence the coding process to generate certain predictive analytics in a way that will advance its own interests. After all, the AI's coder or supplier would likely be sensitive to the wishes of those purchasing the software. This conflict of interest is similar to that which exists when a company engages proxy advisors for services. In this manner, there is an element of human responsibility in the design of AI, even if an AI director is appointed to the board. Second, insofar as the AI software periodically requires updated data to be fed into it, management can selectively feed certain data sets and omit others. Thus, even if AI directors become a reality, they could not completely eliminate directorial or managerial liability on the part of responsible human beings who have influenced the process of design, as long as human agents are responsible for the selection, purchase, maintenance, and operation of the AI machine" (as per Chiu and Lim).

Conclusion

I trust that this walk on the wild side did not go beyond a semblance of sanity or reason.

Today's world does not seem quite ready for AI board members. Whether tomorrow's world will welcome AI board members is a matter we can only speculate about. The AI would have to be leaps and bounds better than the AI we presently have. Assuming that AI could be advanced to that level of facility, we might indeed find ourselves facing a competition between appointing human board members versus AI board members to corporate boards.

May the competition be fair and balanced.

Note: *For supplemental materials depicting the aspects discussed in this chapter, refer to Appendix B, which contains various augmented diagrams, charts, and additional related facets of relevance.*

CHAPTER 22
AI & LAW: FORMAL VERIFICATION

Key briefing points about this article:

- AI is increasingly being used throughout societal applications
- Much of the AI is being pell-mell rushed into being fielded
- A lack of dutiful verification and validation (V&V) is widespread
- Lawyers are going to be brought in and asked to deal with unsavory AI
- We provide herein a brief overview of formal verification in the computing realm

Introduction

In your lawyering capacity, imagine that you have taken on a new client that has gotten into some hot water due to their AI system.

The client is a firm that has crafted an AI system that provides a tremendous capability and the company has quickly gained market share in their industry via leveraging this outsized state-of-the-art innovation which is based on Machine Learning (ML) and Deep Learning (DL). The ML/DL entails computational pattern matching, a facility that has been the underpinning for many of today's best-known AI apps, including the widely heralded Alexa and Siri conversationally interactive systems.

Competitors are being left behind in the dust. The firm has gotten blazing headlines for its clever use of AI, especially since its system embodies algorithmic decision making (ADM). The software is used to render real-time decisions, having replaced the traditional use of human labor. Excitingly, the company is avidly considering going public while the iron is still hot.

So far, so good.

Turns out though that the AI has been caught doing a number of unsavory acts.

The range of untoward actions is somewhat extensive. There are documented instances of the AI seemingly making its algorithmic decisions based on racial biases and gender biases. In addition, outright errors have been detected and the AI has clearly generated obvious and outrageously wrongful erroneous decisions from time to time.

I'd bet that your legal mind is already racing as you quickly assess the situation and can see a zillion legal issues brewing for this firm.

Yes, your legal prowess is desperately needed to aid this client in figuring out the legal issues at stake and try to keep the entire ship from striking a gigantic iceberg (or, has it already?). Speaking of icebergs, the reported issues of the AI system are luckily being kept relatively quiet. The odds are that there is a lot more hidden under the surface and the AI might be riddled with pervasive adverse programming and legally atrocious development practices.

I'm sorry if this seems nightmarish to you. One supposes that having such a client will be at times exhilarating as to the legal import of the matters at hand, counterbalanced by the immense pressures to provide a successful legal path out of their quagmire. Many lawyers would instantly lament that they weren't brought into the fold earlier, much earlier. Anyway, it is what it is, and you are now facing a legal circumstance where the horse is already partially out of the barn.

There is a lot to unpack about the legal underpinnings in this case. I won't be able to cover everything in this short discussion, so let's at least focus on some major facets of fruitful consideration.

Who is to be held responsible for AI that goes astray and performs untoward actions?

The typically knee-jerk answer is that AI is the responsible party. The AI is somehow assumed to embody a semblance of human agency. But, to be clear, we don't have that kind of AI these days. We do not have sentient AI. We don't know if AI sentience is even possible. Claims that the AI has acted of its own will are relatively disingenuous at this time (though, it is hard to predict what the future might hold, which of course the aspirational goal of AI researchers is to someday attain sentient AI).

The gist is that there are humans that set up the AI and put it into use.

Legally, we presumably would seek redress from those that established the AI or are maintaining or otherwise fostering the AI. Companies that have crafted AI systems will need lawyers that know how to internally guide the AI building efforts to minimize AI-arising legal problems down the road (regrettably, that didn't happen in this instance). Firms that have already put forth AI apps are likely to find themselves facing legal wranglings when the AI they've released fails to abide by fairness and allied precepts. That's what this case study illustrates.

For a company like the one depicted in this tale-of-woe legal saga, they are likely to try and deploy a vacuous legal excuse by simply asserting that the AI did it. Many firms using AI have tried that vaunted route, desirous of distracting and redirecting attention toward the AI and ergo shifting the lighthouse beam of intense scrutiny away from themselves.

It would almost seem a plausible form of deniability since society has often been boondoggled into believing that the "computer did it" as though the computer magically had its own mind and soul. The harsh reality is that even the latest of AI is still plain old software and still being devised and fielded by humans at the wheel.

AI In The Law Meets Formal Verification

Shifting gears, lawyers faced with these kinds of AI calamities are often apt to immediately wonder or perhaps directly ask as to what kind of verification was done before the AI was put into active production and allowed to be used in everyday settings.

Let's use that as a springboard to discuss the role of *formal verification* of computing systems.

Generally, the field of computer science includes an entire subfield focused on the formal verification of software and hardware. The overarching idea is to find ways to verify formally (i.e., explicitly, documented, repeatable, explainable, etc.) that a given computer system is provably correct. Another angle is to try and *disprove* that a computer system is correct, thus essentially proving that the computer system is in fact incorrect.

Please be aware that this is a very hard problem to solve. It is also a hugely important matter.

By and large, most of the apps and computers that we rely upon today have never been formally verified per se. There have undoubtedly been attempts at doing verification, but this is usually undertaken on a somewhat hodgepodge basis. Portions of a system might have been tested and examined though not to a fully formalized degree.

Doing a complete end-to-end formalized verification is currently a somewhat narrowly employed approach, usually for a limited or constrained domain such as computer hardware design amid digital circuits but much less so for software (mainly tried in areas such as cryptography, encryption, and so on).

Why is this so hard to do?

The true sense of formal verification entails deriving a kind of formal proof regarding a computer system, doing so for the software, the hardware, or for both.

Envision that we could take a given computer program, including AI, and transform it into the purity of mathematical notation. Based on this mathematical modeling, we now have a viable chance at churning out a formal proof. Think of those math proofs you did in your algebra classes as a visualization of what this proving approach consists of.

Many dozens of formal proof approaches have been devised. The list is lengthy, including finite state machines, automated theorem proving, process algebra, denotational semantics, Hoare logic, and a lot of other means. Sorry to say that there is no silver bullet as yet.

To further clarify, the word "verification" is somewhat being overloaded in this discussion. We all generally accept that verification has to do with verifying something as to its correctness. Those in the depths of formal verification would emphasize that there are two catchwords to be mindful of, namely the *verification* of computer systems and the distinctly different *validation* of computer systems (often referred to as the V&V checking process all-told).

The verification role amounts to the notion that the computer system works correctly with respect to whatever the specification states. This attempts to answer the question as to whether we have managed to make that which we sought out to make.

The validation role tends to ask whether the right thing has been made. Does the computer system actually meet the needs of those that are reliant upon the system? In a sense, this addresses the larger and at times more open-ended aspect of building something that matters.

We are more likely to be able to reasonably pursue the verification aspects in a mathematically robust way than we can do with validation. This is due to the notion that if we have a formal specification of what the computer system is supposed to do, we can then examine the program and compare it to the specification. Either the program fully and completely adheres to the specification, or it does not. If the program does not match the specification, you can formally declare that the program is "incorrect" with respect to the given specification.

Another offshoot of the V&V has to do with the coined *satisfiability* problem.

A research paper discussing the formal verification of AI describes the problem this way: "Formal verification is a very active field in computer science that aims to prove the correctness of a software or hardware systems with respect to specified properties, using mathematical proofs. Two main properties are often investigated: (1) (Un)satisfiability: checking if for a given input, getting a certain output is (not) feasible, (2) Robustness: checking if adding noise to a given input changes its output" (as stated in "Robustness and Explainability of Artificial Intelligence" by Ronan Hamon, Henrik Junklewitz, Igancio Sanchez, *European Commission JRC Technical Report*).

They further indicate that satisfiability and robustness are intertwined: "Verifying the satisfiability property is nonetheless in the majority of cases not possible, as the input space is infinite, and not known. This issue is circumvented by considering instead an evaluation of the robustness of the model at the inputs present in the dataset, as an approximation to the real input space. These methods aim to guarantee that for all points in a neighborhood of a given input, the outputs stay the same" (as per Hamon, Junklewitz, and Sanchez).

Conclusion

Now that you've been dragged through a modicum of an overview of formal verification in computing, you might be mulling over how this relates to that new client and how you are going to legally aid their endeavors.

The gist is that the odds are extremely low that the AI system was subjected to a formal verification process. This can raise the stakes in being able to argue that the firm did whatever it reasonably could do to try and ensure that the AI was going to operate correctly. If they did no verification at all, they would obviously be on precarious ground. If they did some verification, the question arises as to how much and in what manner did they do so. Was it slipshod? Did it abide by commonly accepted practices? Did it strive toward the topmost of accepted practices?

A lawyer that is not particularly versed in computing and nor AI is bound to be taken aback when discovering that their client did not dutifully perform an A-to-Z complete and exhaustive formal verification of their released AI. For any complex form of software or AI, this is not an especially realistic expectation.

Of course, whether you can convince a court or a jury of this outstretched possibility is another matter. In any case, do not fall for those AI developers that tell you that since it isn't viable to do a complete formal verification they resorted to doing none at all. That might some sensible on a wink-wink basis among others in the computer field, but I dare say that legally it won't likely fly.

Good luck on advising that client and may the winds of legal good fortune be on your side.

Note: *For supplemental materials depicting the aspects discussed in this chapter, refer to Appendix B, which contains various augmented diagrams, charts, and additional related facets of relevance.*

CHAPTER 23

AI & LAW: DIFFERENTIAL PRIVACY

Key briefing points about this essay:

- AI is increasingly being used throughout societal applications
- This is partially attributed to the advent of Machine Learning and Deep Learning
- These AI techniques tend to require lots of data for training purposes
- The data used for training might get "memorized" by the AI
- An adverse result could be that the AI violates strict privacy laws

Section 1: Introduction

Let's talk about differential privacy.

Before we do so, perhaps we can start on a somewhat lighter note and cover something of a more carefree consideration.

Have you ever seen a baby duckling that is imprinted on its mother duck?

You certainly must have seen videos, pictures, or perhaps witnessed such imprinting in action. The little baby duckling relentlessly follows the mother duck and won't give up doing so. Everywhere the mother duck goes, the baby duckling is sure to follow.

In case you didn't already know, there is a chance that a baby duckling can imprint on some other creature if, for example, the mother duck is nowhere around when the duckling first engages in imprinting. There have been instances of a duckling imprinting on a dog, a cat, and even on humans. For a real mind-blower, experiments by researchers have shown that a duckling can imprint on objects too, such as a rolling ball or other inanimate items that are able to move around.

I realize that you didn't likely read this discussion wanting to learn about ducklings, but it turns out that the aspect of imprinting is a relevant concept that I'll be bringing you back to in a moment as I discuss the topic of differential privacy.

Please hang onto the imprinting facet.

Meanwhile, let's shift our attention to the heavyweight matter of databases and privacy. Numerous laws about privacy exist in a weblike manner across federal, state, and international jurisdictions. Whereas it used to be the case that just about anybody could put up an online database and fill it with all kinds of personal data about other people, doing so without any semblance of protection for privacy, the laws now can make this rather simple act into either an outright crime or decidedly subject to serious civil legal action.

The initial forays into protecting databases or sets of data often consisted of forcing access to the data to be first screened by some form of login and query system. A user interested in accessing a database had to get approval to do so, and once so approved would receive a traceable login.

Whenever an approved user made a query into the database, the system would check to see if the user should be shown the requested data.

Another means of somewhat protecting a dataset and offering provisions for privacy consists of the data being available only via reporting mechanisms. You might not be able to see a specific record and instead can only get aggregated or summarized reporting about the data. The idea was that a summary lumps everyone together and ergo would seem to protect against seeing any specific record and intruding on the privacy of a particular person.

The thing is, all of those precautions are still vulnerable to privacy intrusions.

For example, a tricky way to potentially subvert the privacy of an aggregated or summarized reporting system is to do enough reports that you might be able to triangulate your way to a specific record or particular person. You ask for a summary of all the people in the database. You then ask for a summary of the people over the age of 65. You then ask for a summary of those that are single. And so on. You can then use those summaries to calculate the particulars of one person, doing so by the fact that they were included in some of the summaries and excluded in the others. It is a mathematical puzzle though one that can often be sneakily carried out.

There is an ongoing cat-and-mouse game between those that want to crack into private data and those that want to protect it.

This brings us to another means of trying to protect data, namely a technique known as *differential privacy*. The notion is straightforward. We can use mathematical techniques to purposely add "noise" to the data so that the real data is kept hidden from inspection. When you get a summarized or aggregated report from the database, it contains the additional "noise" such that you can no longer readily pinpoint any specific individual or record.

You could say that we are adding randomly to the data to embellish it. This masks the real data and confounds attempts to isolate the real data. We aren't though truly being random per se, in the sense that we want to add data or indications that are at least representative of the underlying data. I say this because otherwise, the "noise" is going to undercut our ability to make sense of the data all-told.

If you have a database that contains data about one person that is a redhead and nine that have blond hair, we have to be careful about the "noise" that is being added for the summary reports. For example, if we have the system automated differentiator opt to (essentially) make up new data that has four people that are redheads, we would no longer be able to analyze the true proportion of those that are redheaded versus those that are blonds. As such, there needs to be a smarter or more representative way to create this fake data that can simultaneously hide the real data from privacy intrusions.

One of our main goals would be to reduce the probability that someone running an indefinite number of summary reports could triangulate their way to the real data. A common way to tell a system how much differentiation you want as the administrator responsible for the database would to be adjust a metric typically referred to as the epsilon. By lowering or raising the epsilon value, you can instruct the system to add a lot of noise or just a modicum of noise when queries or summaries are generated.

Realize that there is a tradeoff between having a lot of noise being added and yet still allowing for the database to be used reliably and sensibly. Any attempt to analyze the various patterns within the data, such as when examining opinion surveys, could be rendered untenable if the noise levels are relatively high. Any conclusions you are drawing about the data would be potentially askew due to the noise that has been added (depending on the quality of the noise-producing functionality).

I trust that this seems clear-cut and you can see how handy differential privacy can be.

AI In The Law And Differential Privacy

Our next shift in direction entails discussing AI.

You might be aware that the recent advent of AI has been partially fueled by the use of Machine Learning (ML) and Deep Learning (DL). Machine Learning and Deep Learning consist of a form of computational pattern matching that relies extensively or entirely on data. The notion is that data is fed into an ML/DL algorithm for training purposes. Mathematical patterns are presumably discovered in the data and this becomes the means for the computer to then, later on, do akin pattern detection in freshly presented data.

The typical scenario is this. We assemble a dataset or database of data that will be used to train our ML/DL algorithms. The data is usually fed unfettered into the Machine Learning facility and the ML/DL mathematically analyzes the data to try and find computationally discoverable patterns. After finding computational patterns, we can then turn loose the ML/DL and make use of it in everyday activities. The ML/DL is no longer accessing the original data, having been disconnected from it once the training has been completed.

I don't want to be the bearer of bad news, but there is a sobering wrinkle in this.

Remember the discussion about the baby duckling and the act of imprinting?

We can now put that to good use. The ML/DL can sometimes do a bit of imprinting or what some refer to as "memorization" in that the originally fed-in data can end up being retained in the mathematical model. In other words, even though we remove the original dataset and the ML/DL no longer is accessing it, there is a chance that the model itself has memorized a piece or portion and thus the ML/DL now has that within its confines.

The problem is that the ML/DL could then reveal a considered private portion or piece of the original dataset, doing so "inadvertently" in that the AI developer might be entirely unaware that the ML/DL has landed on that specific imprinting and is now openly revealing it.

What are we to do about this potential AI ML/DL privacy intrusion?

One answer is that we could apply differential privacy to the dataset that is used to train Machine Learning.

During the training process, we make sure that the system differentiator is adding noise to the data being fed into the ML/DL that is being trained. This would tend to mitigate the chances of the ML/DL memorizing a specific piece of data that is real. Note that the ML/DL might nonetheless still do some memorization or imprinting, but at least going to be the noise-added data and not the real data itself.

A helpful report by the European Commission concerning various emerging AI issues describes differential privacy this way: "Differential privacy consists in adding noise to the training data to reduce the influence of each individual sample on the output. The implementation introduced in differential privacy for deep learning consists in adding noise to the gradients at each iteration of the iterative training algorithm. It provides probabilistic guarantees on the level of privacy reached by a model, i.e., how hard it is to retrieve the actual training data from the model. It acts as a regularization technique, and in this respect, it prevents overfitting but also may greatly reduce the performances of the systems in terms of accuracy if the level of privacy is too high. Differential privacy comes in addition of additional measures to increase the level of protection, such as preventing the direct access to the parameters of the models, and limiting the number of queries an adversary might be able to do on a system" (as per the JRC Technical Report on "Robustness and Explainability of Artificial Intelligence" by Ronan Hamon, Henrik Junklewitz, and Ignacio Sanchez).

Legal and ethical AI matters arise when building and deploying AI systems, including the possibility that the AI will violate privacy provisions. Differential privacy when used for an AI system can provide some privacy-inducing assistance.

Conclusion

Suppose you have a client that you are providing legal services. They have set up an AI system that uses Machine Learning. The data used for the establishment of the AI system is based on data that contains various clearly private-oriented data. It needs to be legally protected.

The client is soon going to make the AI system available in the marketplace.

As their lawyer, I'm sure that you would want to counsel them to be mindful of ensuring that the AI doesn't violate any privacy protection provisions.

I'd bet that the AI developers might scoff at the possibility of any privacy intrusions by the AI since they would exhort that the database used to train the AI is quite behind-the-scenes and the AI is completely disconnected from the database due to having completed the training process.

Believe it or not, the AI developers might be unfamiliar with the aspect that some ML/DL algorithms can end up memorizing or imprinting on the originally fed data. Even if the AI developers are vaguely aware of the notion, they probably did not do any closeup inspection to try and detect whether the ML/Dl has in fact gone that route.

You might want to ask them whether they had considered using differential privacy during the build of the AI system. This could make the difference between a released AI that is going to violate privacy laws or not doing so.

Furthermore, if your client, later on, does get accused of violating privacy protections, you are bound to have a stronger legal case based on having used differential privacy rather than not having done so.

Those AI developers might have skirted around the hard stuff to get the AI sooner out the door, though this will assuredly look bad in the eyes of the court and a jury.

Note: *For supplemental materials depicting the aspects discussed in this chapter, refer to Appendix B, which contains various augmented diagrams, charts, and additional related facets of relevance.*

CHAPTER 24
AI & LAW: DISRUPTIVE IMPACTS

Key briefing points about this essay:

- AI is increasingly being used throughout societal applications
- Many depict AI as being a disruptive technology
- The impression perhaps being a big-bang form of disruption
- A more measured view posits a handy three-part framework
- We explore this in AI business adoption and corporate law impacts

Section 1: Introduction

Many are describing AI as a type of disruptive technology.

You might wonder whether the use of the word "disruptive" is profoundly on-target or being excessively overblown. In today's world, it often seems that just about anything and everything is readily labeled as outsized, outstretched, and somehow categorically disruptive. The ratcheting up of outlandish superlatives about what is happening can be a bit disconcerting, especially so when it comes to advanced technologies.

Every new technology is seemingly heralded as a new beginning or a world upending cataclysmic entrant.

An interesting and measured exploration of AI as a disruptive technology in the context of corporate law was undertaken by Iris Chiu and Ernest Lim, doing so in the *Berkeley Law Journal* via a published piece entitled "Technology vs Ideology: How Far Will Artificial Intelligence Transform Corporate Governance and Business?" (Volume 18, Issue 1, 2021).

They posit that AI will decidedly impact corporate governance, business processes, business practices, and otherwise permeate and alter all manner of organizational and managerial elements of modern-day businesses. That being said, they also emphasize that in the near future there does not seem to be any foundational changes and that instead, we ought to anticipate a more so incremental emergence of AI impacts.

This is a handy and nuanced way to contemplate the advent of AI-related disruption.

In other words, rather than taking at face value that the word "disruption" implies an all-out explosive and somewhat instantaneous altering of our existence, we can take a more nuanced view of the matter. It is reasonable to envision that at times a new technology might be mildly disruptive, substantively disruptive, or whole-hog disruptive. There isn't a necessity to jump right away to the most radical and extremely impactful variant of disruption.

Their three-part analytical framework provides a series of levels to illuminate how disruption can range from mild to foundational. We can take a close look at the three proposed levels and see how they relate to the disruptive nature of AI as applied to corporate governance and correspondingly corporate law.

AI As A Disrupting Influence In Corporations

The naming of the three levels is instructive and almost self-evident in their respective meanings:

1. Incremental/facilitative
2. Radical/disruptive
3. Fundamental/structural

Let's tackle each of the levels, one at a time.

As per the researchers: "The first level, 'incremental/facilitative' means that technological change largely facilitates well-accepted business purposes, such as growth, cost-savings, and other efficiencies."

We are all pretty much expecting that the adoption of AI in business will aid in serving new markets and producing new or improved goods. This will lead to notable growth, particularly in sectors that can best initially leverage AI capabilities. We can also expect the arising of goods or services that heretofore were not at all possible without the adoption of AI. Think of autonomous vehicles and self-driving cars as one such instance.

There is also the belief that AI will reduce the labor needed for the production of goods or the delivery of services. Chatbots that are using AI will take on service-oriented tasks. Assembly plants and manufacturing will increasingly deploy robots that are using AI. All of these AI infusions are going to presumably carry with them a lowered cost of doing business.

Those are expected advantages from AI. At the same time, there isn't any earth-shattering impact that AI of that nature will have on businesses, industries, and economies all-told. You would be hard-pressed to make the case that this AI usage is a wholescale ideological change from how businesses generally operate today.

You are probably thinking, well, there must be more disruption that AI can bring about.

This brings us to the researcher's second level: "The second level of the framework we propose, 'radical/disruptive' change, begins with technological change as a 'challenger' that attains a 'substitutive' character."

That appears to be subdued, so let's take a deeper look, per the researchers: In this manner, we characterize radical/disruptive' change as a marked manner of change in organizing and conducting economic life, where such change develops from an emerging 'new way of doing things' that becomes a challenger to, and eventually substitute for, the conventional 'way of doing things.' We also regard radical/disruptive change as likely to give rise to questions regarding institutional or paradigm change, *i.e.*, whether existing institutions in the law can allow for such a change, and whether existing paradigms have shifted, or need to shift, in response."

Now we are veering into a resemblance of disruption that seems more befitting with the usual characterization of that which is claimed as disruptive.

One such example would be something that almost seems impossible to imagine. Envision that a board of directors adds an AI system as a member of the board. Duly elected by shareholders, we now have AI side-by-side with human board members. You could refer to this AI as a "robot" but that might be somewhat jarring and also regrettably misleading. We don't necessarily need a classic walking and talking robot to be a board member. Akin to using Alexa or Siri, the AI board member could be an online system that is merely accessed via a speaker and microphone, embodied within an electronic device or a conventional-looking computer system.

This example kicks into gear the corporate legal impacts of AI infusion. Would the AI be construed as having a legal personality or agency, akin to human board members? What kind of liability would be associated with this AI board member? Would existing regulations pertaining to boards and board members still be viable in the case of AI board membership, or would we need to change such laws?

If you are somewhat taken aback by the AI board member notion, note that we aren't as yet to the third level of disruption.

Here's what the researchers say about the third level: "Finally, we introduce the third level of our framework, 'fundamental/structural' change, which refers to completely new and eradicative ways of organizing or conducting economic life, such that conventional structures and institutions are largely replaced, much like how urbanization replaces and therefore eradicates old rural ways of life in a geographical area."

To some degree, this third level might smack of inconceivable sci-fi style changes. The furthest reaching viewpoint entails envisioned AI that entirely runs, manages, and operates corporations. The research proffers this imagery: "Such AI would be programmed to serve the founder's purposes and could execute contracts with third parties or carry out actions and deals based on coded instructions dependent on the fulfillment of pre-determined conditions."

Conclusion

One supposes you could take an even larger step and suggest that rather than only having humans as the corporate legal person to establish a firm, AI does that too. We could have an AI-founded company, which is then run and operated by AI. That almost seems reasonable, especially if compared to an AI-founded company that is run and operated by both AI and humans. We would seem to loathe to envisage humans working under the stern thumb and probing managerial eye of AI.

Terminology being floated about this far-reaching use of AI in business is that we would exist in an AI-controlled economic universe. We would have taken techno-capitalism to its most extreme position. Putting on your lawyering cap, it would seem abundantly obvious that prevailing corporate laws and governance norms would be turned on their heads.

Lawyers should gird themselves for the lighter yet still significant legal changes that will arise at level one, and keep an eye on level two, while perhaps holding their breath to see whether we truly inch our way to level three. The laws of today might be like the proverbial tale of the frog in the boiling pot of water. Initially, it all seems to be going along sufficiently, adjusting little by little, but in the end, the impacts emerge as a massive and overwhelming change.

Note: *For supplemental materials depicting the aspects discussed in this chapter, refer to Appendix B, which contains various augmented diagrams, charts, and additional related facets of relevance.*

CHAPTER 25
AI & LAW: STEALING MACHINE LEARNING

Key briefing points about this essay:

- AI is increasingly being used throughout societal applications
- Much of this AI is based on Machine Learning and Deep Learning
- Suppose someone opts to reverse engineer the AI
- They could set up their own version (cheaply, quickly) or attack the AI
- Significant legal and ethical AI concerns arise

Introduction

A company approaches you for your esteemed legal advice.

Turns out that this firm has spent gobs of time and money developing an AI system that is aiming to disrupt an entire industry.

So far, they have managed to craft an AI-based Machine Learning (ML) and Deep Learning (DL) model that does quite amazing analyzes and produces fast real-time algorithmic decisions that seem to surpass that of human decision-makers.

The company is subsisting on venture capital monies and has not yet become profitable. To try and see if their AI is good enough for marketplace usage, they tentatively made it available to the public and are collecting feedback. Assuming all goes well, they soon hope to formally release the AI system, making a big splash as they do so, and shortly thereafter will eagerly seek to launch their IPO (initial public offering) while the getting is good.

Everything seems cheery.

Here's though what has happened and serves as the basis for wanting your legal insights. Upon making the budding prototype or pilot of their AI available, they soon noticed that another firm a few days later posted an AI system that appeared suspiciously similar. This was a shocker. How in the world did someone else craft nearly an identical AI system, coincidently releasing it at the same point in time as them?

The odds were ostensibly astronomical. The AI developers in the firm that first put forth the AI knew just about everyone else pursuing similar capabilities. No one else was close to getting their AI as far along. A newcomer out of the blue being able to attain the same AI was unimaginable.

When the initial shock wore off, the firm thought that perhaps someone internally had leaked the AI system. It would be relatively easy to have an insider of the firm sneakily share a copy of the AI system with outsiders. An internal investigation got underway. To the surprise of top management, there seemed to be absolutely no indication that a traitorous insider opted to provide others with the AI system.

The only other plausible explanation would seem to be that the firm must have had a breach of its cybersecurity protections. An outsider must have snaked their way through multiple levels of very tight cyber barriers and grabbed up a copy of the AI system. Those dastardly thieves!

That would abundantly be construed as theft, they assumed, and sought your legal acumen about the legal recourse available to them. They wanted to pursue criminal charges and a civil lawsuit against the offending company. Throw the book at them, they exclaimed to you.

At first glance, this might seem like an everyday computer-related theft case. Nothing extraordinary. Breaches and the stealing of software are a common occurrence these days.

Let's add a twist.

Suppose that there wasn't any breach of cyber security. Imagine that the other firm did not lay a finger on breaking in or hacking to obtain the AI system. Nonetheless, they somehow appear to have ended up with the AI.

How did they do it? Was it one of those infamous locked room mysteries whereby there seems to be no logical explanation for how the AI was seemingly replicated?

The answer to how the AI was replicated is rooted in a bit of technological trickery and raises some interesting legal and ethical AI questions. We next examine and reveal the mysterious magic of how a rabbit was pulled out of a hat.

Get yourself ready for the big reveal.

Claimed Stealing Of Machine Learning Models

Let's set the stage for how an AI system could be "stolen" and yet not be whole hog copied or have a copy lifted from the purveyor of the AI.

In this instance, the AI was making use of Machine Learning and Deep Learning. These are simply algorithms that undertake computational pattern matching. You first select which ML/DL algorithms you want to use (there are plenty of choices). Next, you assemble a large trove of data to ostensibly "train" the ML/DL. You see, the data that is fed into the ML/DL is crunched through to mathematically find any discoverable patterns.

Once those computationally found patterns are relatively settled, you can then put the AI into use. Thus, when fed new data, the ML/DL will rely upon the earlier discovered patterns and seek to find those patterns in the new data. Think of facial recognition as an example of ML/DL. The ML/DL is trained on faces and then, later on, can potentially identify the faces of people in a crowd.

Machine Learning and Deep Learning are the darlings of the AI world today. The vaunted capabilities of Alexa and Siri can be placed at the feet of ML/DL. By and large, most of the AI that you hear about, see, or experience is probably under-the-hood making use of ML/DL.

When a trained ML/DL is put into use, a typical approach consists of disconnecting the ML/DL from the original training data. You keep the training data hidden away, well-protected from any prying eyes. Generally, there is no need for the ML/DL to have access to the original data now that it has been trained on it.

The guts of the ML/DL embody whatever computational patterns were findable.

You might put the ML/DL into action and make it available to outsiders by setting it up on a cloud service. This is referred to as Machine Learning as a Service (MLaaS). People that are supposed to be able to use the AI system can access it via cloud hosting. You might require that users sign-up and get a login, or you could just make the AI openly available for use. For an added layer of protection, the use of SMPC (secure multi-party computation) and other akin protections might also be set up.

Okay, so we've got this AI system using ML/DL that was trained on a dataset and the original training data is hidden away. The ML/DL model now encapsulates the algorithm and all of its various settings that represent the patterns found in the original dataset.

How can this AI be lifted if you say that it won't or can't be obtained whole-hog copied?

Believe it or not, one such approach entails merely running the ML/DL and cleverly attempting to reverse engineer what the algorithm is (based on seeing the outputs as per the inputs that you provide while running the ML/DL), and ascertain what the settings of the algorithm are. You might not be able to gauge everything to an exhaustive degree, but you could potentially use whatever clues you find to then put together a new ML/DL that closely resembles the one that you are reverse engineering.

In case you think that perhaps this would be onerous, such that the outsider might have to expend a great deal of time and effort to figure this out, the reality is that depending upon the complexity of the ML/DL chosen, this can be done at times without extraordinary costs or delays. As stated by researchers that have examined such matters: "It is possible for adversaries to passively extract the private models even if they are protected by SMPC, using known and newly devised model extraction attacks. We show that our attacks are not only theoretically possible but also practically feasible and cheap, which makes them lucrative to financially motivated attackers such as competitors or customers" (as stated by Robert Reith, Thomas Schneider, and Oleksandr Tkachenko, "Efficiently Stealing Your Machine Learning Models" as published in the WPES 2019 Conference proceedings).

To give you a flavor for how easily this can be performed, here's a case study that the researchers undertook and the somewhat startling results thereof: "We show that it is possible to extract a highly accurate model using only 854 queries with the estimated cost of $0.09 on the Amazon ML platform, and our attack would take only 7 minutes over the Internet" (per Reith, Schneider, and Tkachenko).

Please note that your mileage will vary. Various factors come to play and it could be costly or time-consuming to do this type of reverse engineering. You have to take into account the original ML/DL models chosen, the setup aspects, and the like. That being said, you could reasonably contend that most of today's ML/DL systems being actively used are somewhat easier to crack and sitting ducks, as it were.

Returning to the earlier depicted scenario, imagine that it might have taken months upon months to set up an ML/DL, obtain the needed data, painstakingly train the ML/DL, all of which required an immense amount of developer time and resources. The costs could be in the millions or more of dollars. And then, upon making the ML/DL available for use, it is essentially probed without much cost or time required, and then readily replicated by some outsider. The outsider then sets up their own ML/DL that has "leveraged" all the hard work and costly investment, doing so on the heels of your more elaborate and expensive path to attain the AI.

This form of "attack" is known as an exploratory attack. Researchers define this attack as follows: "Exploratory attacks, which our paper further explores, intend to unravel information about the algorithm's configuration, or general inner workings, in order to extract the algorithm or its parameters, to find weaknesses in the algorithm, or to gain knowledge useful for further attacks, such as evasion attacks" (per Reith, Schneider, and Tkachenko).

One vital aspect to keep in mind is that though an attacker might do this to replicate the AI, there are other insidious possibilities. By knowing how the ML/DL works, it is theoretically feasible to then get the ML/DL to take actions that perhaps are untoward or unsavory. This could harm those that are otherwise innocently using the ML/DL. An attacker might also find ways to get the ML/DL to benefit themselves, perhaps sending them money or other valuable items.

Per the ongoing game of cat and mouse in the cyber security realm, there are ways to try and detect and curtail these attacks or misappropriations (if we are to coin it that way).

For example, oftentimes such an attack requires that the ML/DL be invoked over and over again, wherein the attacker sends waves of data as input and then records the outputs produced. Assuming that any ordinary user would not be using the ML/DL in this massively repeated fashion, you can detect that queries are being repeatedly submitted. The repetitive nature of queries might be a telltale clue of an attack and the AI system might then refuse the queries. Etc.

Conclusion

Let's discuss the ethical AI facets.

An apparent assertion is that ethically this attempt to reverse engineer or force a reveal of an ML/DL is inherently wrong. The original developer put in the time and effort, and someone is ripping them off. Dastardly.

Of course, suppose that this was an ML/DL that was purposely set up to do bad things, to begin with. Not all AI is necessarily built for the veritable *AI For Good* aspirations. It could be that this is *AI For Bad*, set up by bad hat actors or evildoers, and perhaps the revealing of the inner elements would aid in overturning or coping with the foulness of the ML/DL.

From a legal perspective, there are plenty of questions that arise too.

Let's go back to the earlier sketched scenario. The "attacker" did not copy the ML/DL (well, one supposes you can argue the meaning of the word "copy"). They did not break into the AI system. They did not cause direct harm to the AI system, meaning that they did not alter the ML/DL or try to make it do unsavory acts.

They might argue that all they did was run the ML/DL, which apparently was made available for that very purpose, namely to allow users to run it. The fact that they observed the inputs and outputs, and then later opted to craft "their own" ML/DL, does not mean that they crossed any legal lines (they would presumably contend).

Suppose the company that set up the ML/DL had required a licensing agreement that any users cannot do this kind of reverse engineering. Would that aid the legal case that the other company "stole" the IP (Intellectual Property) of their ML/DL? Counterarguments are readily made to this claim. We can also ponder whether the revealing of mere settings or parameters is credibly construed as legal IP.

You could even try to argue that if the ML/DL was made available to repeated queries and there wasn't any attempt made to detect or deflect those efforts, perhaps the company that set up the AI system allowed this kind of activity to occur. They insufficiently protected their AI.

Round and round it goes.

The only thing we can say for sure about these AI-related matters is that attorneys are going to be needed to sort through the legal issues. On top of that, new laws about AI systems are in the midst of being crafted and instituted. Lawyers are needed for those efforts too.

Once those laws are implemented, you can bet that lawyers will need to be sufficiently AI-savvy to contend with the myriad of legal landmines and gotchas that will arise.

Note: *For supplemental materials depicting the aspects discussed in this chapter, refer to Appendix B, which contains various augmented diagrams, charts, and additional related facets of relevance*

APPENDIX A
TEACHING WITH THIS MATERIAL AND BIBLIOGRAPHY

The essays in this book can readily be used as a reading supplemental to augment traditional textbook-oriented content, particularly used in a class on AI or a class about the law.

Courses where this material is most likely applicable encompass classes at a college or university level.

Here are some typical settings that might apply:

- Computer Science. Classes studying AI, or possibly a CS social impacts class, etc.
- Law. Law classes exploring technology and its adoption for legal uses.
- Sociology. Sociology classes on the adoption and advancement of technology.

Specialized classes at the undergraduate and graduate level can also make use of this material.

For each chapter, consider whether you think the chapter provides material relevant to your course topic.

There are plenty of opportunities to get the students thinking about the topics and encourage them to decide whether they agree or disagree with the points offered and positions taken.

I would also encourage you to have the students do additional research beyond the chapter material presented (I provide next some suggested assignments that they can do).

RESEARCH ASSIGNMENTS ON THESE TOPICS

Your students can find research and background material on these topics, doing so in various tech journals, law journals, and other related publications.

Here are some suggestions for homework or projects that you could assign to students:

a) Assignment for foundational AI research topics: Research and prepare a paper and a presentation on a specific aspect of AI, such as Machine Learning, ANN, etc. The paper should cite at least 3 reputable sources. Compare and contrast to what has been stated in the chosen chapter.

b) Assignment for Law topics: Research and prepare a paper covering Law aspects via at least 3 reputable sources and analyze the characterizations. Compare and contrast to what has been stated in the chosen chapter.

c) Assignment for a Business topic: Research and prepare a paper and a presentation on businesses and advanced technology regarding AI and Law. What is trending, and why? Make sure to cite at least 3 reputable sources. Compare and contrast to the depictions herein.

d) Assignment to do a Startup: Have the students prepare a paper or business plan about how they might start up a business in this realm. They could also be asked to present their business plan and should also have a prepared presentation deck to coincide with it.

You can certainly adjust the aforementioned assignments to fit your particular needs and class structure.

You'll notice that I usually suggest that (at least) 3 reputable cited sources be utilized for the paper writing-based assignments.

I usually steer students toward "reputable" publications, since otherwise, they will cite some less reliable sources that have little or no credentials, other than that they happened to appear online was easy to retrieve. You can, of course, define "reputable" in whatever way you prefer, for example, some faculty think Wikipedia is not reputable while others believe it is reputable and allow students to cite it.

The reason that I usually ask for at least 3 citations is that if the student only relies upon one or two citations, they usually settle on whatever they happened to find the fastest. By requiring 3 (or more) citations, it usually seems to inspire them to explore more extensively and likely end-up finding five or more sources, and then whittling it down to 3 if so needed.

I have not specified the length of their papers and leave that to you to tell the students what you prefer.

For each of those assignments, you could end up with a short one to two-pager or you could do a dissertation length in-depth paper. Base the length on whatever best fits for your class, and likewise the credit amount of the assignment within the context of the other grading metrics you'll be using for the class.

I usually try to get students to present their work, in addition to doing the writing. This is a helpful practice for what they will do in the business world. Most of the time, they will be required to prepare an analysis and present it. If you don't have the class time or inclination to have the students present their papers, then you can presumably omit the aspect of them putting together presentations.

GUIDE TO USING THE CHAPTERS

For each of the chapters, I provide the next some various ways to use the chapter contents.

You can assign the below tasks as individual homework assignments, or the tasks can be used for team projects. You can easily layout a series of assignments, such as indicating that the students are to do item "a" below for say Chapter 1, then "b" for the next chapter of the book, and so on.

a) What is the main point of the chapter and describe in your own words the significance of the topic.

b) Identify at least two aspects in the chapter that you agree with and support your concurrence by providing at least one other outside researched item as support; make sure to explain your basis for agreeing with the aspects.

c) Identify at least two aspects in the chapter that you disagree with and support your disagreement by providing at least one other outside researched item as support; make sure to explain your basis for disagreeing with the aspects.

d) Find an aspect that was not covered extensively in the chapter, doing so by conducting outside research, and then offer an expanded indication about how that aspect ties into the chapter, along with the added significance it brings to the topic.

e) Interview a specialist in the industry about the topic of the chapter, collect from them their thoughts and opinions, and readdress the chapter by citing your source and how they compared and contrasted to the material,

f) Interview a relevant professor or researcher in a college or university setting about the topic of the chapter, collect from them their thoughts and opinions, and readdress the chapter by citing your source and how they compared and contrasted to the material,

g) Try to update a chapter by finding out the latest on the topic and ascertain whether the issue or topic has now been solved or whether it is still being addressed, explain what you come up with.

The above are all ways in which you can get the students of your class involved in considering the material of a given chapter. You could mix things up by having one of those above assignments per each week, covering the chapters over the course of the semester or quarter.

SUGGESTED REFERENCES TO EXPLORE

To help get your students started in finding relevant and important papers on the topic of AI and the law, I provide next a handy bibliography that can be utilized.

You could also assign the students to each (or in teams) read an assigned reference from the list, and then have them provide either a written summary and review or do so as part of a classroom presentation.

BIBLIOGRAPHIC REFERENCES

1. Aleven, Vincent (1997). "Teaching Case-Based Argumentation Through a Model and Examples," Ph.D. Dissertation, University of Pittsburgh.

2. Aleven, Vincent (2003). "Using Background Knowledge in Case-Based Legal Reasoning: A Computational Model and an Intelligent Learning Environment," Artificial Intelligence.

3. Amgoud, Leila (2012). "Five Weaknesses of ASPIC+," Volume 299, Communications in Computer and Information Science (CCIS).

4. Antonious, Grigoris, and George Baryannis, Sotiris Batsakis, Guido Governatori, Livio Robaldo, Givoanni Siragusa, Ilias Tachmazidis (2018). "Legal Reasoning and Big Data: Opportunities and Challenges," August 2018, MIREL Workshop on Mining and Reasoning Legal Texts.

5. Ashley, Kevin (1991). "Reasoning with Cases and Hypotheticals in HYPO," Volume 34, International Journal of Man-Machine Studies.

6. Ashley, Kevin, and Karl Branting, Howard Margolis, and Cass Sunstein (2001). "Legal Reasoning and Artificial Intelligence: How Computers 'Think' Like Lawyers," Symposium: Legal Reasoning and Artificial Intelligence, University of Chicago Law School Roundtable.

7. Baker, Jamie (2018). "A Legal Research Odyssey: Artificial Intelligence as Disrupter," Law Library Journal.

8. Batsakis, Sotiris, and George Baryannis, Guido Governatori, Illias Tachmazidis, Grigoris Antoniou (2018). "Legal Representation and Reasoning in Practice: A Critical Comparison," Volume 313, Legal Knowledge and Information Systems.

9. Bench-Capon, Trevor (2004). "AGATHA: Automation of the Construction of Theories in Case Law Domains," January 2004, Legal Knowledge and Information Systems Jurix 2004, Amsterdam.

10. Bench-Capon, Trevor (2012). "Representing Popov v Hayashi with Dimensions and Factors," March 2012, Artificial Intelligence and Law.

11. Bench-Capon, Trevor, and Givoanni Sartor (2003). "A Model of Legal Reasoning with Cases Incorporating Theories and Values," November 2013, Artificial Intelligence.

12. Breuker, Joost (1996). "A Functional Ontology of Law," October 1996, ResearchGate.

13. Bruninghaus, Stefanie, and Kevin Ashley (2003). "Combining Case-Based and Model-Based Reasoning for Predicting the Outcome of Legal Cases," June 2003, ICCBR'03: Proceedings of the 5th International Conference on Case-based reasoning: Research and Development.

14. Buchanan, Bruce, and Thomas Headrick (1970). "Some Speculation about Artificial Intelligence and Legal Reasoning," Volume 23, Stanford Law Review.

15. Chagal-Feferkorn, Karni (2019). "Am I An Algorithm or a Product: When Products Liability Should Apply to Algorithmic Decision-Makers," Stanford Law & Policy Review.

16. Douglas, William (1948). "The Dissent: A Safeguard of Democracy," Volume 32, Journal of the American Judicature Society.

17. Dung, P, and R. Kowalski, F. Toni (2006). "Dialectic Proof Procedures for Assumption-Based Admissible Argumentation," Artificial Intelligence.

18. Eliot, Lance (2020). AI And Legal Reasoning Essentials. LBE Press Publishing.

19. Eliot, Lance (2020). Artificial Intelligence and LegalTech Essentials. LBE Press Publishing.

20. Eliot, Lance (2020). "FutureLaw 2020 Showcases How Tech is Transforming The Law, Including the Impacts of AI," April 16, 2020, Forbes.

21. Erdem, Esra, and Michael Gelfond, Nicola Leone (2016). "Applications of Answer Set Programming," AI Magazine.

22. Gardner, Anne (1987). Artificial Intelligence and Legal Reasoning. MIT Press.

23. Genesereth, Michael (2009). "Computational Law: The Cop in the Backseat," Stanford Center for Legal Informatics, Stanford University.

24. Ghosh, Mirna (2019). "Automation of Legal Reasoning and Decision Based on Ontologies," Normandie Universite.

25. Grabmair, Matthias (2017). "Predicting Trade Secret Case Outcomes using Argument Schemes and Learned Quantitative Value Effect Tradeoffs," IJCAI June 12, 2017, London, United Kingdom.

26. Hage, Jaap (1996). "A Theory of Legal Reasoning and a Logic to Match," Volume 4, Artificial Intelligence and Law.

27. Hage, Jaap (2000). "Dialectical Models in Artificial Intelligence and Law," Artificial Intelligence and Law.

28. Hage, Japp, and Ronald Leenes, Arno Lodder (1993). "Hard Cases: A Procedural Approach," Artificial Intelligence and Law.

29. Hobbes, Thomas (1651). The Matter, Form, and Power of a Common-Wealth Ecclesiasticall and Civil.

30. Holmes, Oliver (1897). "The Path of the Law," Volume 10, Harvard Law Review.

31. Katz, Daniel, and Michael Bommarito, Josh Blackman (2017). "A General Approach for Predicting the Behavior of the Supreme Court of the United States," April 12, 2017, PLOS ONE.

32. Kowalski, Robert, and Francesca Toni (1996). "Abstract Argumentation," AI-Law96.

33. Laswell, Harold (1955). "Current Studies of the Decision Process: Automation Creativity," Volume 8, Western Political Quarterly.

34. Libal, Tomer, and Alexander Steen (2019). "The NAI Suite: Drafting and Reasoning over Legal Texts," October 15, 2019, arXiv.

35. Lipton, Zachary (2017). "The Mythos of Model Interpretability," March 6, 2017, arXiv.

36. Martin, Andrew, and Kevin Quinn, Theodore Ruger, Pauline Kim (2004). "Competing Approaches to Predicting Supreme Court Decision Making," December 2014, Symposium on Forecasting U.S. Supreme Court Decisions.

37. McCarty, Thorne (1977). "Reflections on TAXMAN: An Experiment in Artificial Intelligence and Legal Reasoning," January 1977, Harvard Law Review.

38. Modgil, Sanjay, and Henry Prakken (2013). "The ASPIC+ Framework for Structured Argumentation: A Tutorial," December 16, 2013, Argument & Computation.

39. Mowbray, Andrew, and Philip Chung, Graham Greenleaf (2019). "Utilising AI in the Legal Assistance Sector," LegalAIIA Workshop, ICAIL, June 17, 2019, Montreal, Canada.

40. Parasuraman, Raja, and Thomas Sheridan, Christopher Wickens (2000). "A Model for Types and Levels of Human Interaction with Automation," May 2000, IEEE Transactions on Systems, Man, and Cybernetics.

41. Popple, James (1993). "SHYSTER: A Pragmatic Legal Expert System," Ph.D. Dissertation, Australian National University.

42. Prakken, Henry, and Giovanni Sartor (2015). "Law and Logic: A Review from an Argumentation Perspective," Volume 227, Artificial Intelligence.

43. Rissland, Edwina (1988). Artificial Intelligence and Legal Reasoning: A Discussion of the Field and Gardner's Book," Volume 9, AI Magazine.

44. Rissland, Edwina (1990). "Artificial Intelligence and Law: Stepping Stones to a Model of Legal Reasoning," Yale Law Journal.

45. Searle, John (1980). "Minds, Brains, and Programs," Volume 3, Behavioral and Brain Sciences.

46. Sunstein, Cass (2001). "Of Artificial Intelligence and Legal Reasoning," University of Chicago Law School, Public Law and Legal Theory Working Papers.

47. Sunstein, Cass, and Kevin Ashley, Karl Branting, Howard Margolis (2001). "Legal Reasoning and Artificial Intelligence: How Computers 'Think' Like Lawyers," Symposium: Legal Reasoning and Artificial Intelligence, University of Chicago Law School Roundtable.

48. Surden, Harry (2014). "Machine Learning and Law," Washington Law Review.

49. Surden, Harry (2019). "Artificial Intelligence and Law: An Overview," Summer 2019, Georgia State University Law Review.

50. Valente, Andre, and Joost Breuker (1996). "A Functional Ontology of Law," Artificial Intelligence and Law.

51. Waltl, Bernhard, and Roland Vogl (2018). "Explainable Artificial Intelligence: The New Frontier in Legal Informatics," February 2018, Jusletter IT 22, Stanford Center for Legal Informatics, Stanford University.

52. Wittgenstein, Ludwig (1953). Philosophical Investigations. Blackwell Publishing.

APPENDIX B
SUPPLEMENTAL FIGURES AND CHARTS

For the convenience of viewing, supplemental figures and charts related to the topics discussed are shown on the next pages

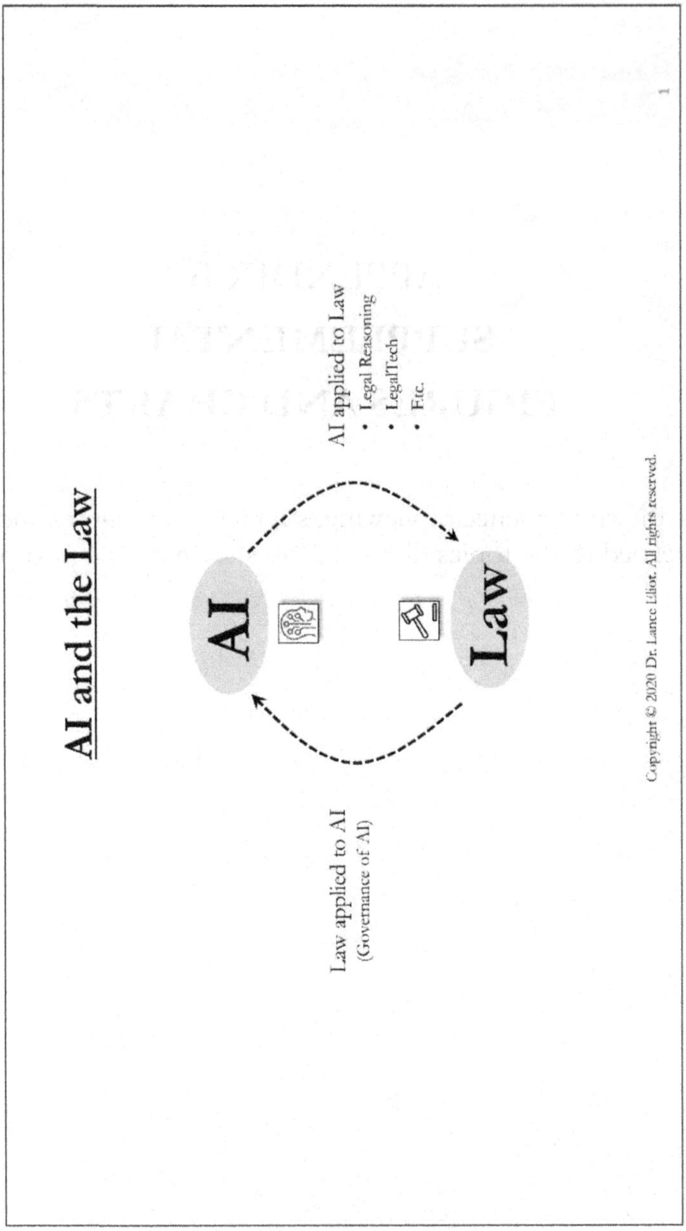
AI and the Law
AI
Law
AI applied to Law
• Legal Reasoning
• LegalTech
• Etc.
Law applied to AI
(Governance of AI)
Copyright © 2020 Dr. Lance Eliot. All rights reserved.
1

Figure 1

AI & Law: Levels of Autonomy For AI Legal Reasoning (AILR)

Level	Descriptor	Examples	Automation	Status
0	No Automation	Manual, paper-based (no automation)	None	De Facto - In Use
1	Simple Assistance Automation	Word Processing, XLS, online legal docs, etc.	Legal Assist	Widely In Use
2	Advanced Assistance Automation	Query-style NLP, ML for case prediction, etc.	Legal Assist	Some In Use
3	Semi-Autonomous Automation	KBS & ML/DL for legal reasoning & analysis, etc.	Legal Assist	Primarily Prototypes & Research Based
4	AILR Domain Autonomous	Versed only in a specific legal domain	Legal Advisor (law fluent)	None As Yet
5	AILR Fully Autonomous	Versatile within and across all legal domains	Legal Advisor (law fluent)	None As Yet
6	AILR Superhuman Autonomous	Exceeds human-based legal reasoning	Supra Legal Advisor	Indeterminate

Figure 1: AI & Law - Autonomous Levels by Rows

Source Author: Dr. Lance B. Eliot

V1.3

Figure 2

AI & Law: Levels of Autonomy For AI Legal Reasoning (AILR)

	Level 0	Level 1	Level 2	Level 3	Level 4	Level 5	Level 6
Descriptor	No Automation	Simple Assistance Automation	Advanced Assistance Automation	Semi-Autonomous Automation	AILR Domain Autonomous	AILR Fully Autonomous	AILR Superhuman Autonomous
Examples	Manual, paper-based (no automation)	Word Processing, XLS, online legal docs, etc.	Query-style NLP, ML for case prediction, etc.	KBS & ML/DL for legal reasoning & analysis, etc.	Versed only in a specific legal domain	Versatile within and across all legal domains	Exceeds human-based legal reasoning
Automation	None	Legal Assist	Legal Assist	Legal Assist	Legal Advisor (law fluent)	Legal Advisor (law fluent)	Supra Legal Advisor
Status	De Facto – In Use	Widely In Use	Some In Use	Primarily Prototypes & Research-based	None As Yet	None As Yet	Indeterminate

Figure 2: AI & Law - Autonomous Levels by Columns

Source Author: Dr. Lance B. Eliot

V1.3

Figure 3

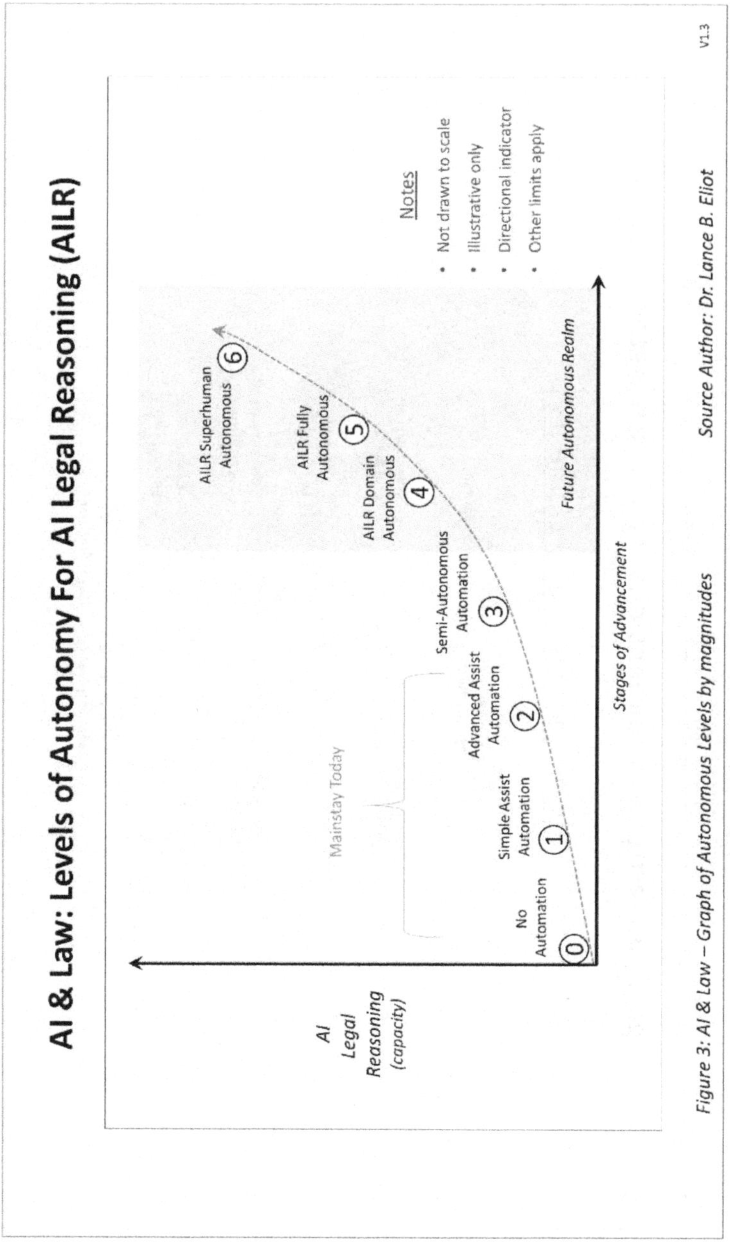
AI & Law: Levels of Autonomy For AI Legal Reasoning (AILR)
AI Legal Reasoning (capacity)
Mainstay Today
0 No Automation
1 Simple Assist Automation
2 Advanced Assist Automation
3 Semi-Autonomous Automation
4 AILR Domain Autonomous
5 AILR Fully Autonomous
6 AILR Superhuman Autonomous
Future Autonomous Realm
Stages of Advancement
Notes
Not drawn to scale
Illustrative only
Directional indicator
Other limits apply
Figure 3: AI & Law – Graph of Autonomous Levels by magnitudes
Source Author: Dr. Lance B. Eliot
V1.3

Figure 4

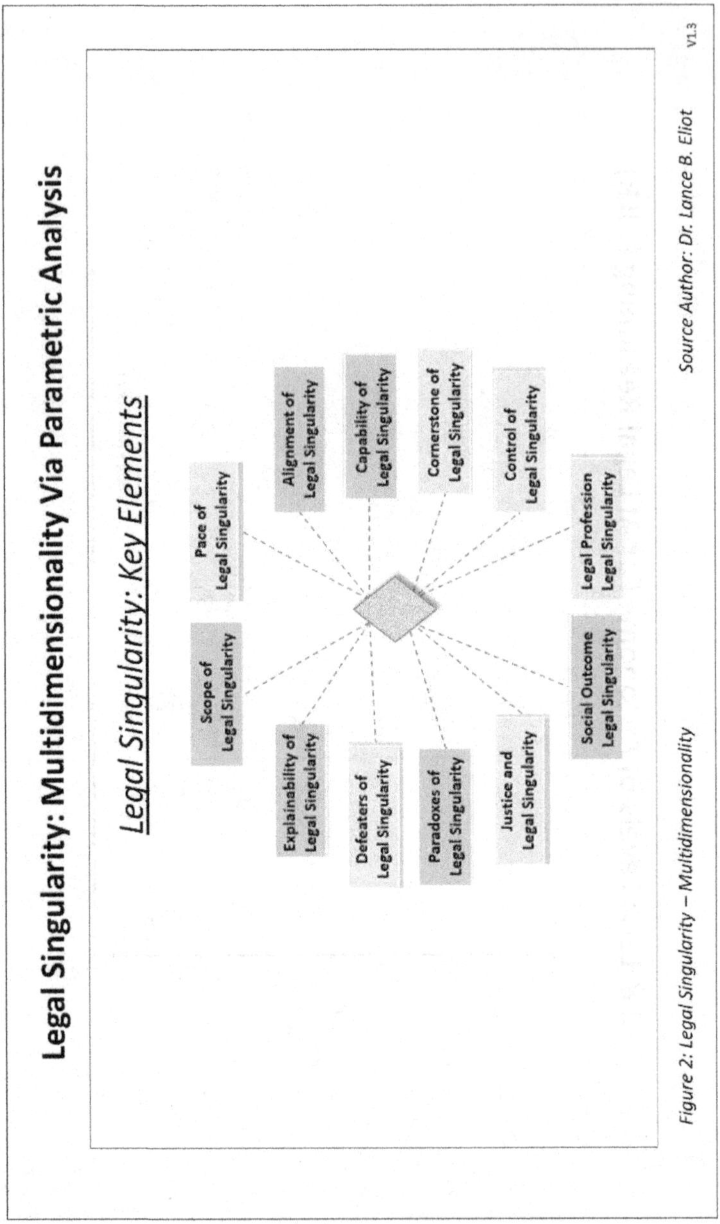
Legal Singularity: Multidimensionality Via Parametric Analysis
Legal Singularity: Key Elements
Scope of Legal Singularity
Pace of Legal Singularity
Explainability of Legal Singularity
Alignment of Legal Singularity
Defeaters of Legal Singularity
Capability of Legal Singularity
Paradoxes of Legal Singularity
Cornerstone of Legal Singularity
Justice and Legal Singularity
Control of Legal Singularity
Social Outcome Legal Singularity
Legal Profession Legal Singularity
Figure 2: Legal Singularity – Multidimensionality
Source Author: Dr. Lance B. Eliot
V1.3

Figure 5

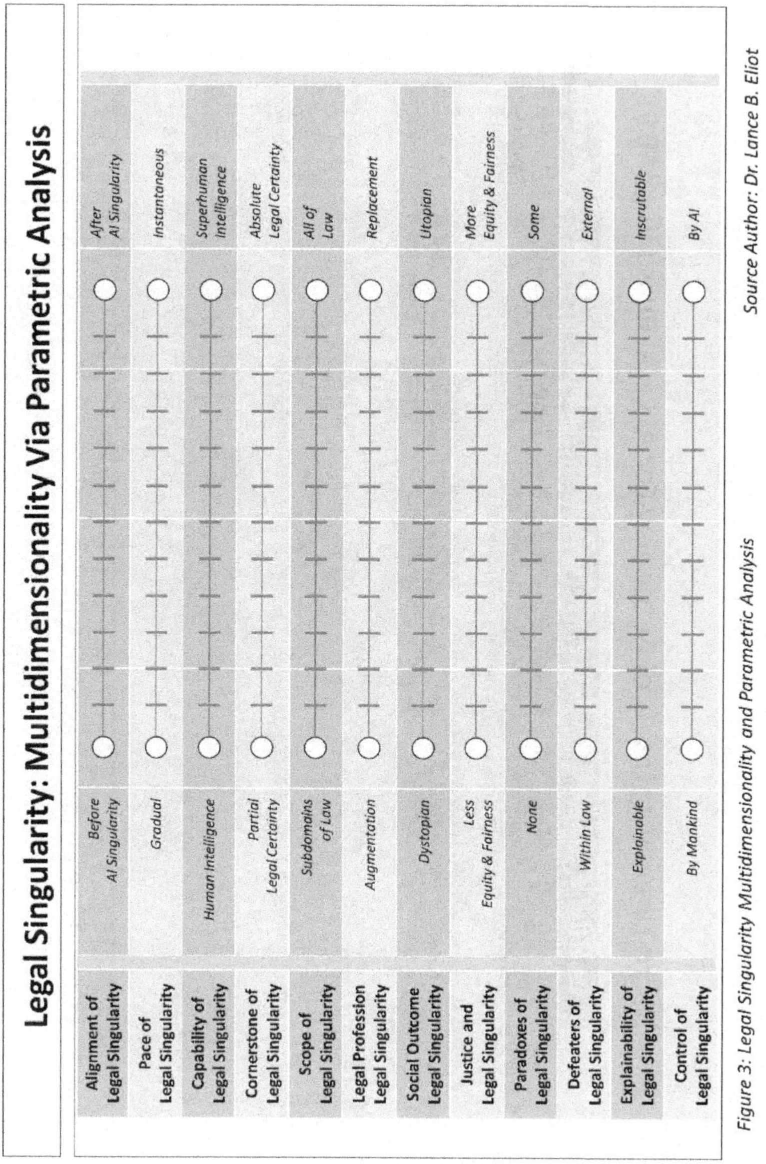

Figure 3: Legal Singularity Multidimensionality and Parametric Analysis

Source Author: Dr. Lance B. Eliot

Figure 6

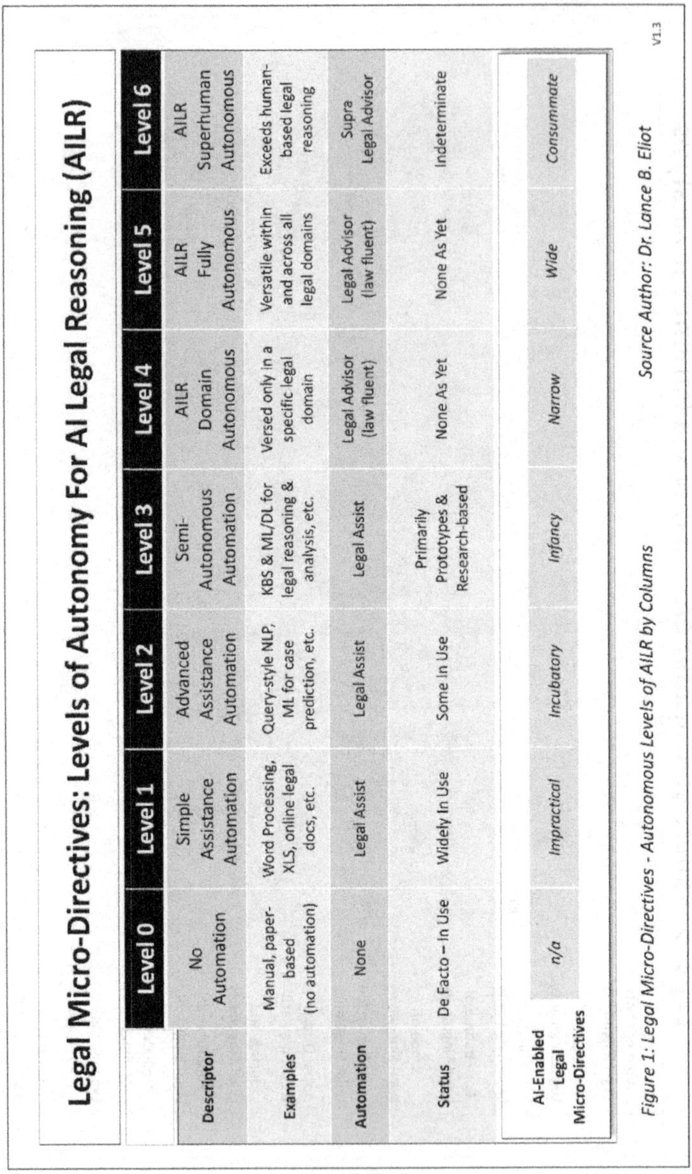

Legal Micro-Directives: Levels of Autonomy For AI Legal Reasoning (AILR)

	Level 0	Level 1	Level 2	Level 3	Level 4	Level 5	Level 6
Descriptor	No Automation	Simple Assistance Automation	Advanced Assistance Automation	Semi-Autonomous Automation	AILR Domain Autonomous	AILR Fully Autonomous	AILR Superhuman Autonomous
Examples	Manual, paper-based (no automation)	Word Processing, XLS, online legal docs, etc.	Query-style NLP, ML for case prediction, etc.	KBS & ML/DL for legal reasoning & analysis, etc.	Versed only in a specific legal domain	Versatile within and across all legal domains	Exceeds human-based legal reasoning
Automation	None	Legal Assist	Legal Assist	Legal Assist	Legal Advisor (law fluent)	Legal Advisor (law fluent)	Supra Legal Advisor
Status	De Facto – In Use	Widely In Use	Some In Use	Primarily Prototypes & Research-based	None As Yet	None As Yet	Indeterminate
AI-Enabled Legal Micro-Directives	*n/a*	*Impractical*	*Incubatory*	*Infancy*	*Narrow*	*Wide*	*Consummate*

Figure 1: Legal Micro-Directives - Autonomous Levels of AILR by Columns

Source Author: Dr. Lance B. Eliot

V1.3

Figure 7

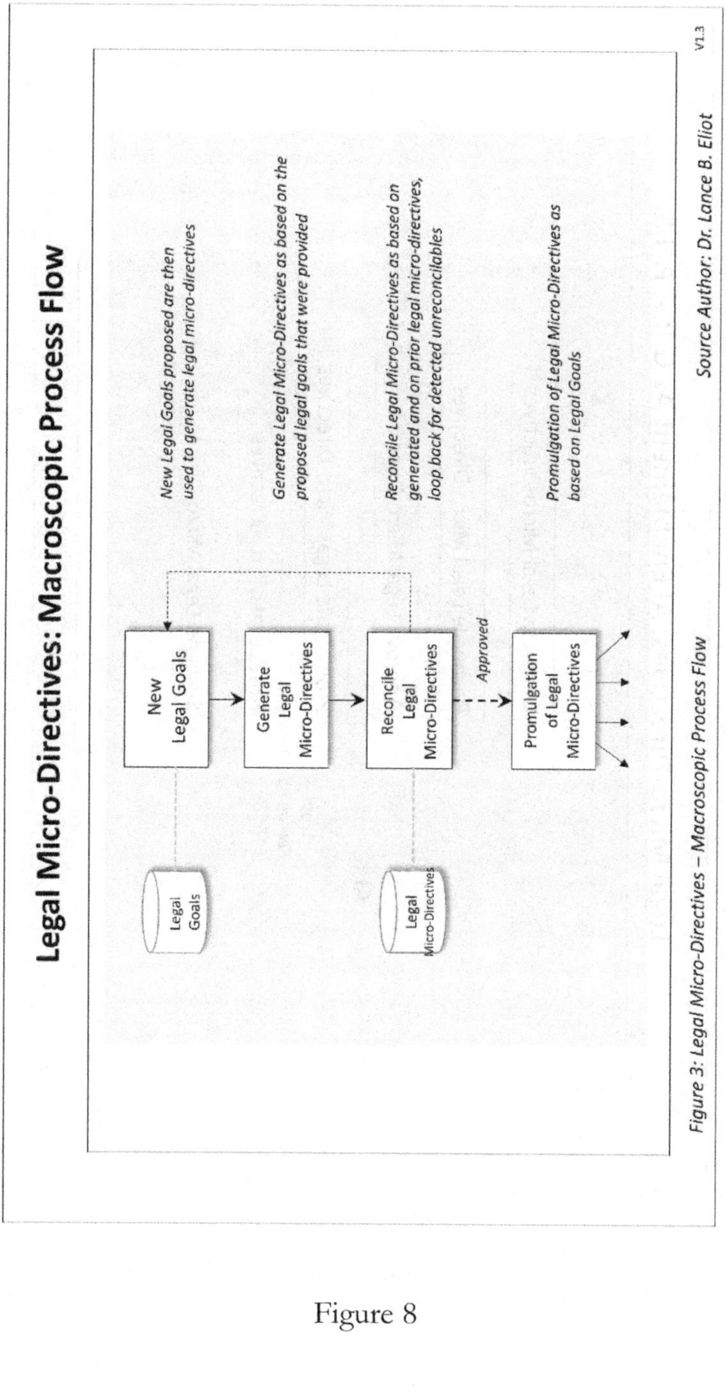
Legal Micro-Directives: Macroscopic Process Flow
Legal Goals
Legal Micro-Directives
New Legal Goals
Generate Legal Micro-Directives
Reconcile Legal Micro-Directives
Approved
Promulgation of Legal Micro-Directives
New Legal Goals proposed are then used to generate legal micro-directives
Generate Legal Micro-Directives as based on the proposed legal goals that were provided
Reconcile Legal Micro-Directives as based on generated and on prior legal micro-directives, loop back for detected unreconcilables
Promulgation of Legal Micro-Directives as based on Legal Goals
Figure 3: Legal Micro-Directives – Macroscopic Process Flow
Source Author: Dr. Lance B. Eliot
V1.3

Figure 8

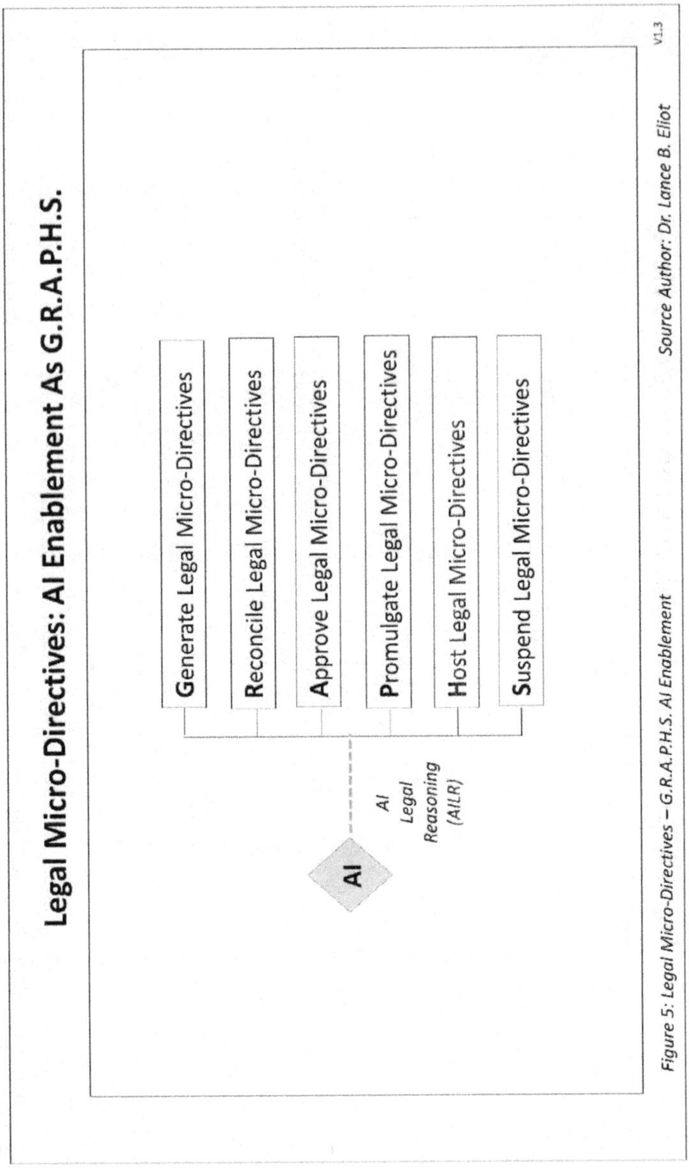
Legal Micro-Directives: AI Enablement As G.R.A.P.H.S.
AI
AI Legal Reasoning (AILR)
Generate Legal Micro-Directives
Reconcile Legal Micro-Directives
Approve Legal Micro-Directives
Promulgate Legal Micro-Directives
Host Legal Micro-Directives
Suspend Legal Micro-Directives
Figure 5: Legal Micro-Directives – G.R.A.P.H.S. AI Enablement
Source Author: Dr. Lance B. Eliot
V1.3

Figure 9

Legal Argumentation: Levels of Autonomy For AI Legal Reasoning (AILR)

	Level 0	Level 1	Level 2	Level 3	Level 4	Level 5	Level 6
Descriptor	No Automation	Simple Assistance Automation	Advanced Assistance Automation	Semi-Autonomous Automation	AILR Domain Autonomous	AILR Fully Autonomous	AILR Superhuman Autonomous
Examples	Manual, paper-based (no automation)	Word Processing, XLS, online legal docs, etc.	Query-style NLP, ML for case prediction, etc.	KBS & ML/DL for legal reasoning & analysis, etc.	Versed only in a specific legal domain	Versatile within and across all legal domains	Exceeds human-based legal reasoning
Automation	None	Legal Assist	Legal Assist	Legal Assist	Legal Advisor (law fluent)	Legal Advisor (law fluent)	Supra Legal Advisor
Status	De Facto – In Use	Widely In Use	Some In Use	Primarily Prototypes & Research-based	None As Yet	None As Yet	Indeterminate
AI-Enabled Legal Argumentation	*n/a*	*Mechanistic (Low)*	*Mechanistic (High)*	*Expressive*	*Domain Fluency*	*Full Fluency*	*Meta-Fluency*

Figure 7: AI Legal Argumentation (AILA) - Autonomous Levels of AILR by Columns *Source Author: Dr. Lance B. Eliot*

V1.3

Figure 10

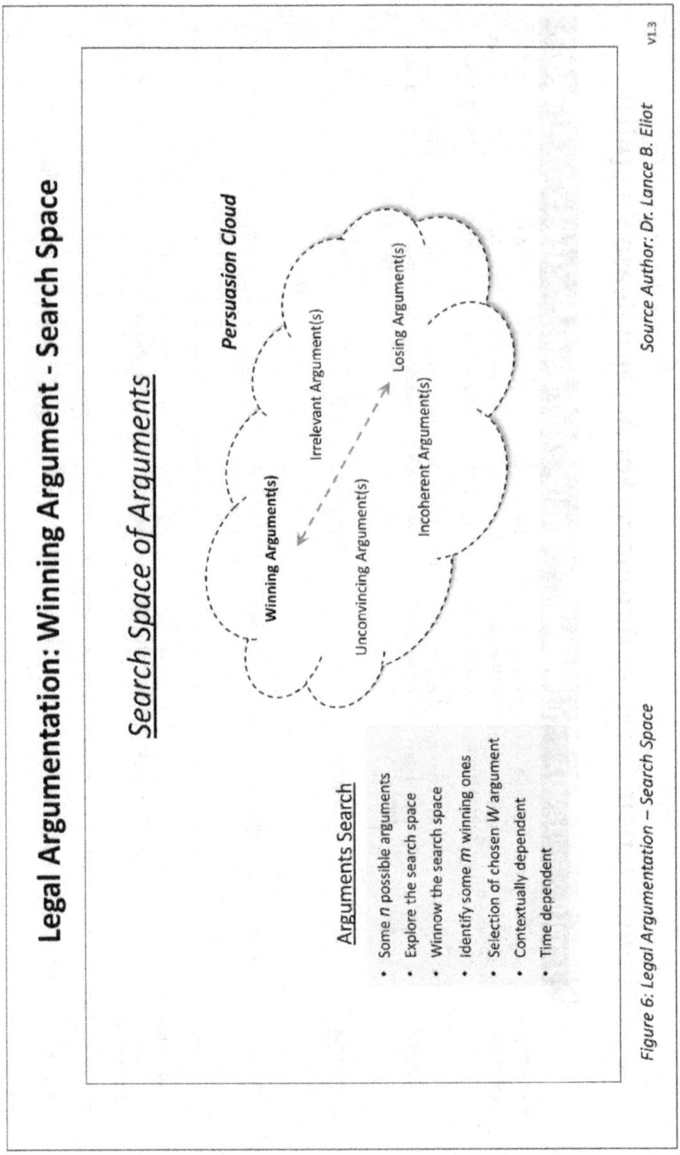
Legal Argumentation: Winning Argument - Search Space
Search Space of Arguments
Persuasion Cloud
Winning Argument(s)
Irrelevant Argument(s)
Losing Argument(s)
Unconvincing Argument(s)
Incoherent Argument(s)
Arguments Search
Some n possible arguments
Explore the search space
Winnow the search space
Identify some m winning ones
Selection of chosen W argument
Contextually dependent
Time dependent
Figure 6: Legal Argumentation – Search Space
Source Author: Dr. Lance B. Eliot
V1.3

Figure 11

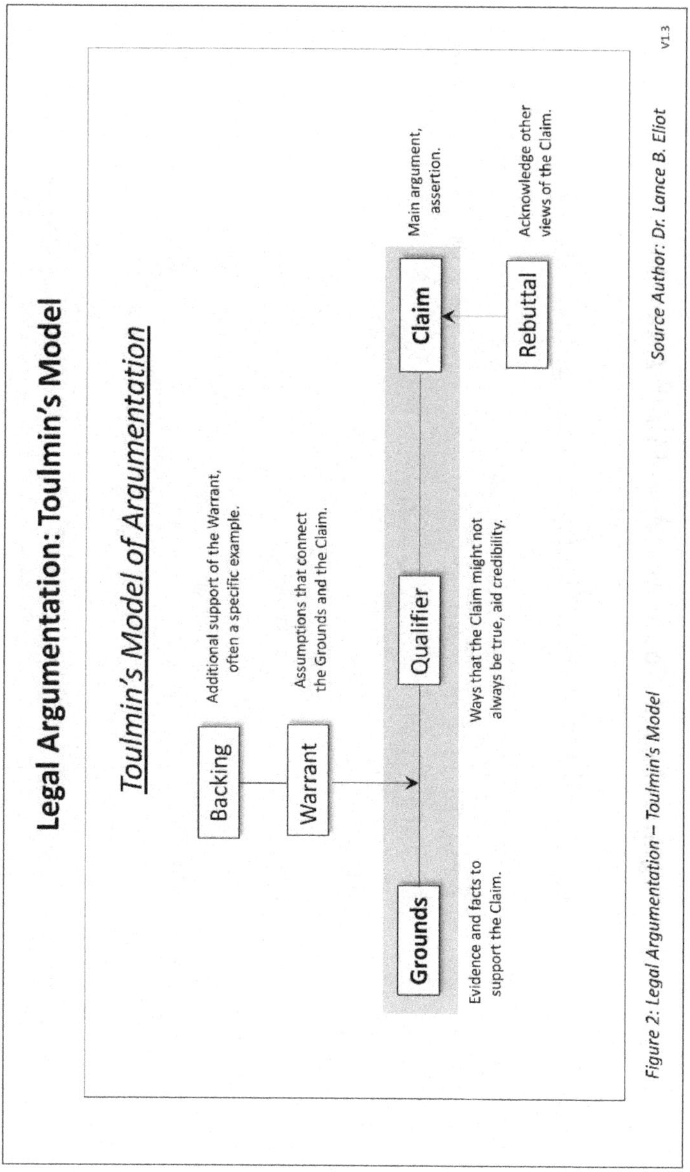
Legal Argumentation: Toulmin's Model
Toulmin's Model of Argumentation
Backing
Additional support of the Warrant, often a specific example.
Warrant
Assumptions that connect the Grounds and the Claim.
Grounds
Evidence and facts to support the Claim.
Qualifier
Ways that the Claim might not always be true, aid credibility.
Claim
Main argument, assertion.
Rebuttal
Acknowledge other views of the Claim.
Figure 2: Legal Argumentation – Toulmin's Model
Source Author: Dr. Lance B. Eliot
V1.3

Figure 12

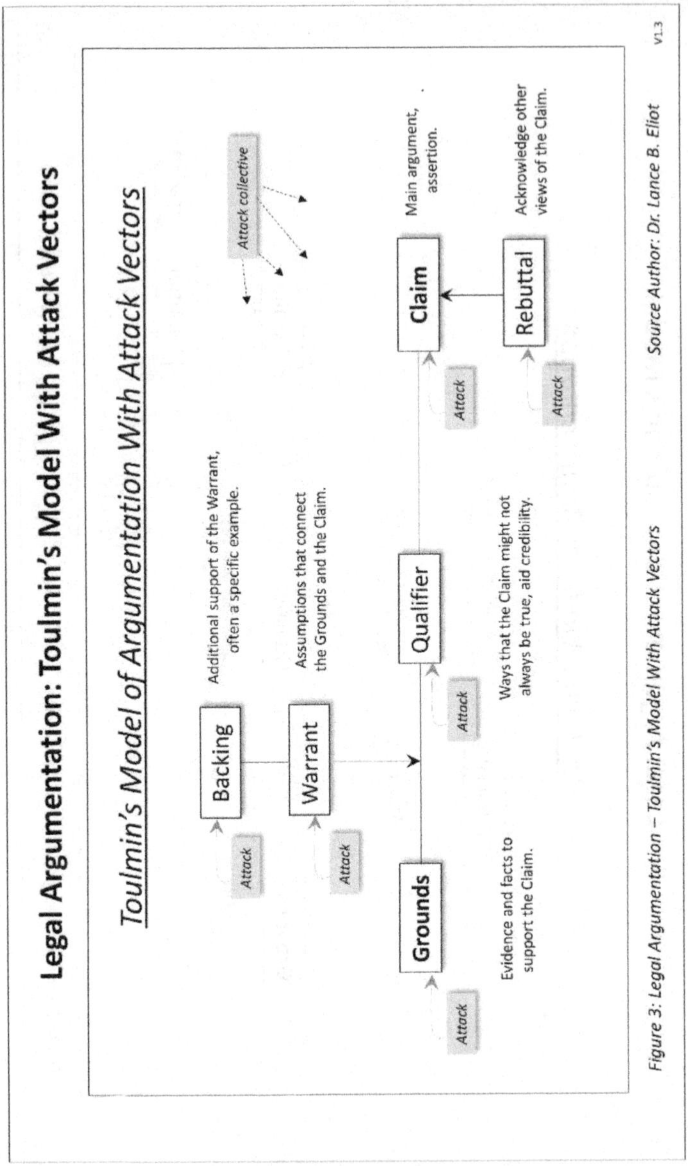
Legal Argumentation: Toulmin's Model With Attack Vectors
Toulmin's Model of Argumentation With Attack Vectors
Attack collective
Backing
Additional support of the Warrant, often a specific example.
Warrant
Assumptions that connect the Grounds and the Claim.
Grounds
Evidence and facts to support the Claim.
Qualifier
Ways that the Claim might not always be true, aid credibility.
Claim
Main argument, assertion.
Rebuttal
Acknowledge other views of the Claim.
Attack
Attack
Attack
Attack
Attack
Attack
Figure 3: Legal Argumentation – Toulmin's Model With Attack Vectors
Source Author: Dr. Lance B. Eliot
V1.3

Figure 13

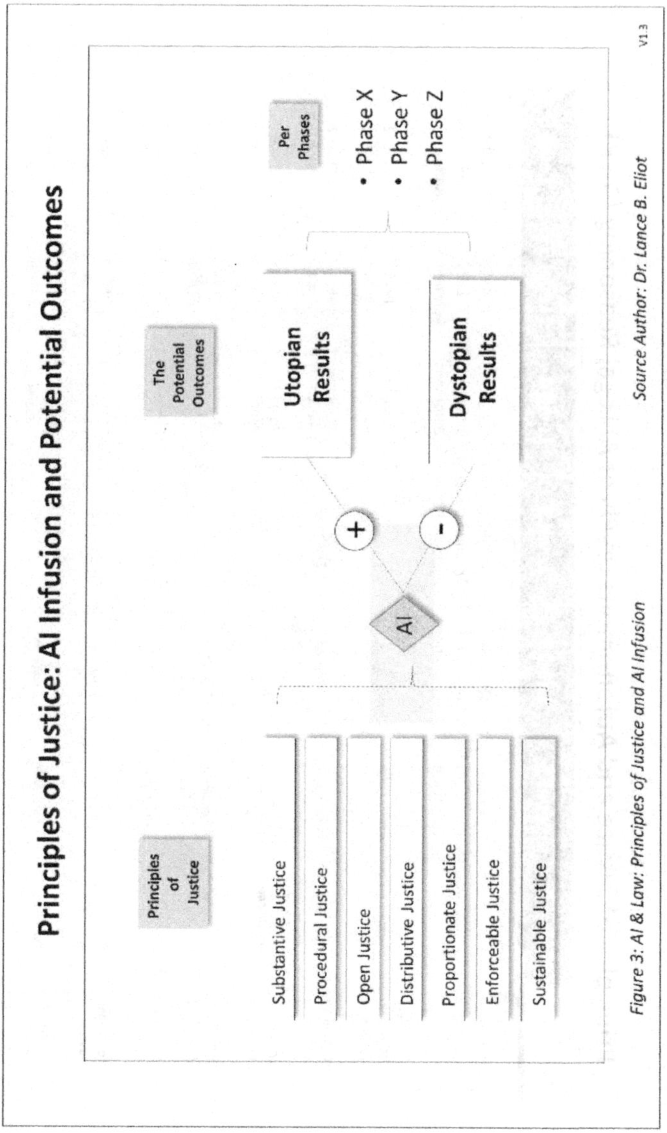
Principles of Justice: AI Infusion and Potential Outcomes
Principles of Justice
Substantive Justice
Procedural Justice
Open Justice
Distributive Justice
Proportionate Justice
Enforceable Justice
Sustainable Justice
AI
+
-
The Potential Outcomes
Utopian Results
Dystopian Results
Per Phases
• Phase X
• Phase Y
• Phase Z
Figure 3: AI & Law: Principles of Justice and AI Infusion
Source Author: Dr. Lance B. Eliot
V1.3

Figure 14

Principles of Justice and Autonomous Levels of AI Legal Reasoning (AILR)

	Level 0	Level 1	Level 2	Level 3	Level 4	Level 5	Level 6
Descriptor	No Automation	Simple Assistance Automation	Advanced Assistance Automation	Semi-Autonomous Automation	AILR Domain Autonomous	AILR Fully Autonomous	AILR Superhuman Autonomous
Substantive Justice	*Traditional*	*Traditional*	*Traditional*	Emerging	Phase X Impacts	Phase Y Impacts	Phase Z Impacts
Procedural Justice	*Traditional*	*Traditional*	*Traditional*	Emerging	Phase X Impacts	Phase Y Impacts	Phase Z Impacts
Open Justice	*Traditional*	*Traditional*	*Traditional*	Emerging	Phase X Impacts	Phase Y Impacts	Phase Z Impacts
Distributive Justice	*Traditional*	*Traditional*	*Traditional*	Emerging	Phase X Impacts	Phase Y Impacts	Phase Z Impacts
Proportionate Justice	*Traditional*	*Traditional*	*Traditional*	Emerging	Phase X Impacts	Phase Y Impacts	Phase Z Impacts
Enforceable Justice	*Traditional*	*Traditional*	*Traditional*	Emerging	Phase X Impacts	Phase Y Impacts	Phase Z Impacts
Sustainable Justice	*Traditional*	*Traditional*	*Traditional*	Emerging	Phase X Impacts	Phase Y Impacts	Phase Z Impacts

Figure 1: AI & Law – Principles of Justice and LoA AILR by Columns

Source Author: Dr. Lance B. Eliot

V1.3

Figure 15

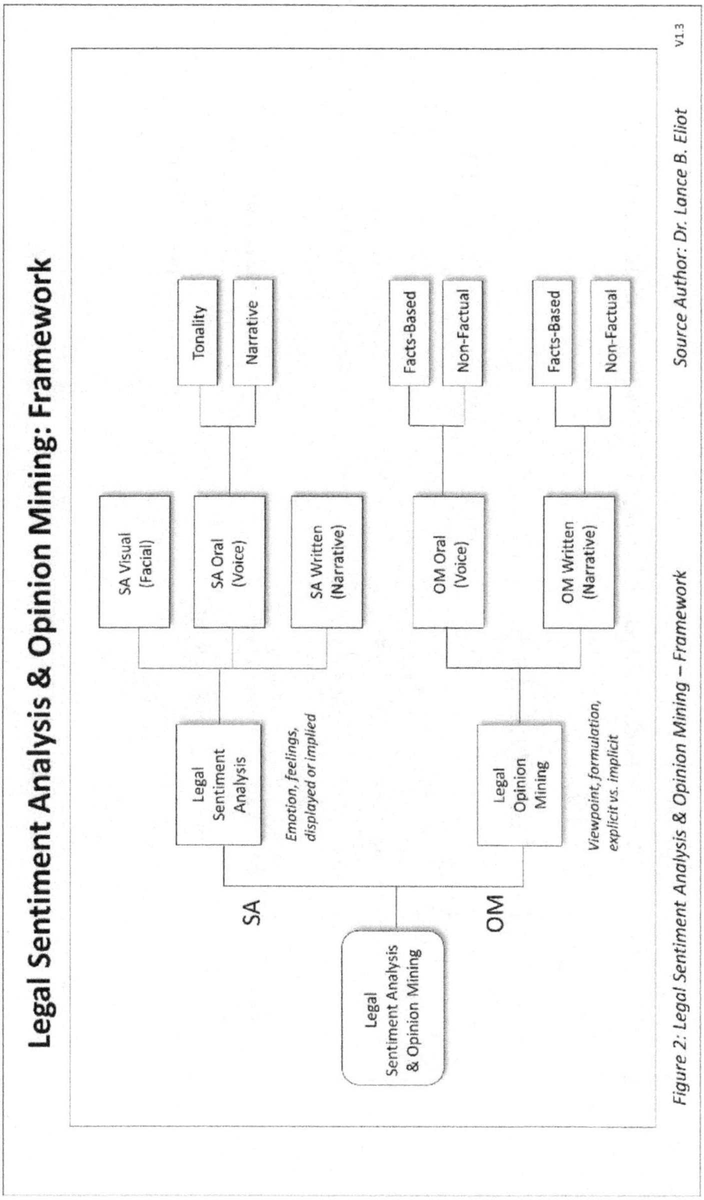
Legal Sentiment Analysis & Opinion Mining: Framework
Legal Sentiment Analysis & Opinion Mining
SA
OM
Legal Sentiment Analysis
Emotion, feelings, displayed or implied
Legal Opinion Mining
Viewpoint, formulation, explicit vs. implicit
SA Visual (Facial)
SA Oral (Voice)
SA Written (Narrative)
OM Oral (Voice)
OM Written (Narrative)
Tonality
Narrative
Facts-Based
Non-Factual
Facts-Based
Non-Factual
Figure 2: Legal Sentiment Analysis & Opinion Mining – Framework
Source Author: Dr. Lance B. Eliot
V13

Figure 16

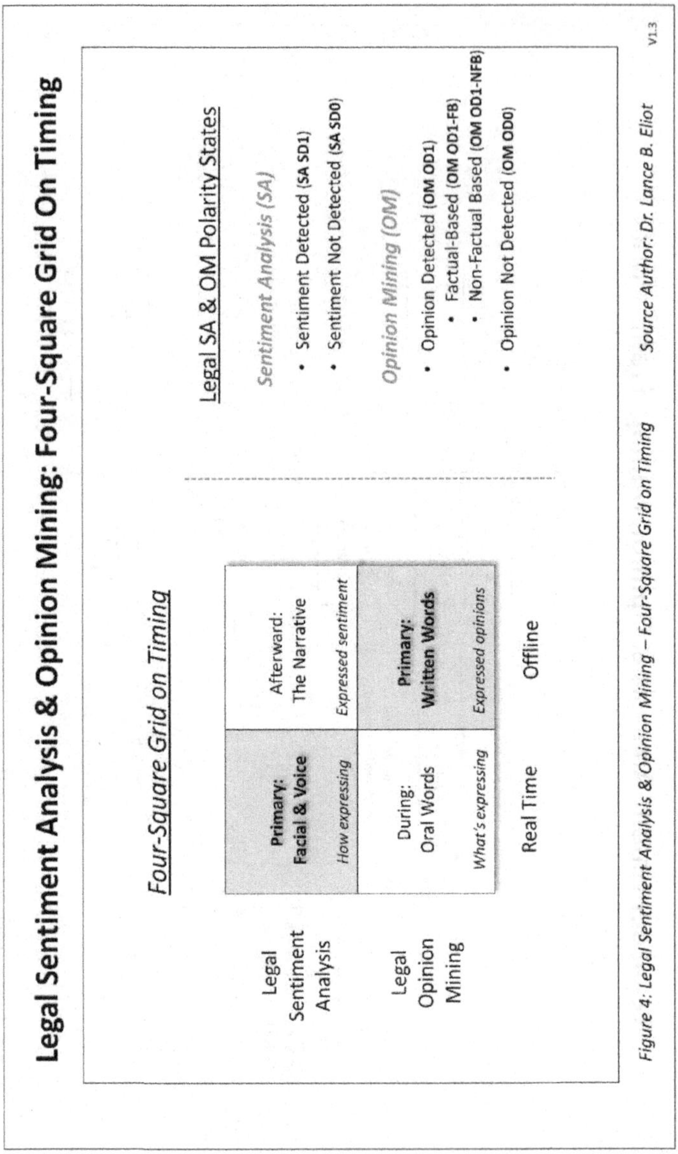
Legal Sentiment Analysis & Opinion Mining: Four-Square Grid On Timing
Four-Square Grid on Timing
Legal Sentiment Analysis
Legal Opinion Mining
Primary: Facial & Voice
How expressing
Afterward: The Narrative
Expressed sentiment
During: Oral Words
What's expressing
Primary: Written Words
Expressed opinions
Real Time
Offline
Legal SA & OM Polarity States
Sentiment Analysis (SA)
Sentiment Detected (SA SD1)
Sentiment Not Detected (SA SD0)
Opinion Mining (OM)
Opinion Detected (OM OD1)
Factual-Based (OM OD1-FB)
Non-Factual Based (OM OD1-NFB)
Opinion Not Detected (OM OD0)
Figure 4: Legal Sentiment Analysis & Opinion Mining – Four-Square Grid on Timing
Source Author: Dr. Lance B. Eliot
V1.3

Figure 17

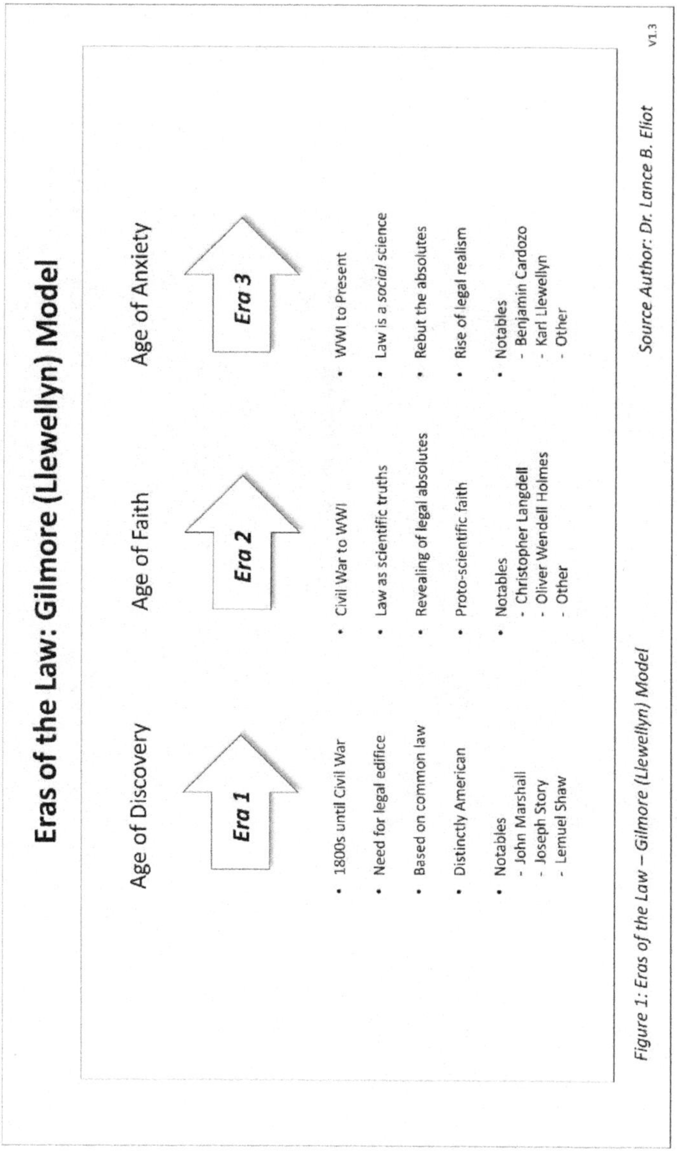
Eras of the Law: Gilmore (Llewellyn) Model
Age of Discovery
Era 1
1800s until Civil War
Need for legal edifice
Based on common law
Distinctly American
Notables
- John Marshall
- Joseph Story
- Lemuel Shaw
Age of Faith
Era 2
Civil War to WWI
Law as scientific truths
Revealing of legal absolutes
Proto-scientific faith
Notables
- Christopher Langdell
- Oliver Wendell Holmes
- Other
Age of Anxiety
Era 3
WWI to Present
Law is a social science
Rebut the absolutes
Rise of legal realism
Notables
- Benjamin Cardozo
- Karl Llewellyn
- Other
Figure 1: Eras of the Law – Gilmore (Llewellyn) Model
Source Author: Dr. Lance B. Eliot
V1.3

Figure 18

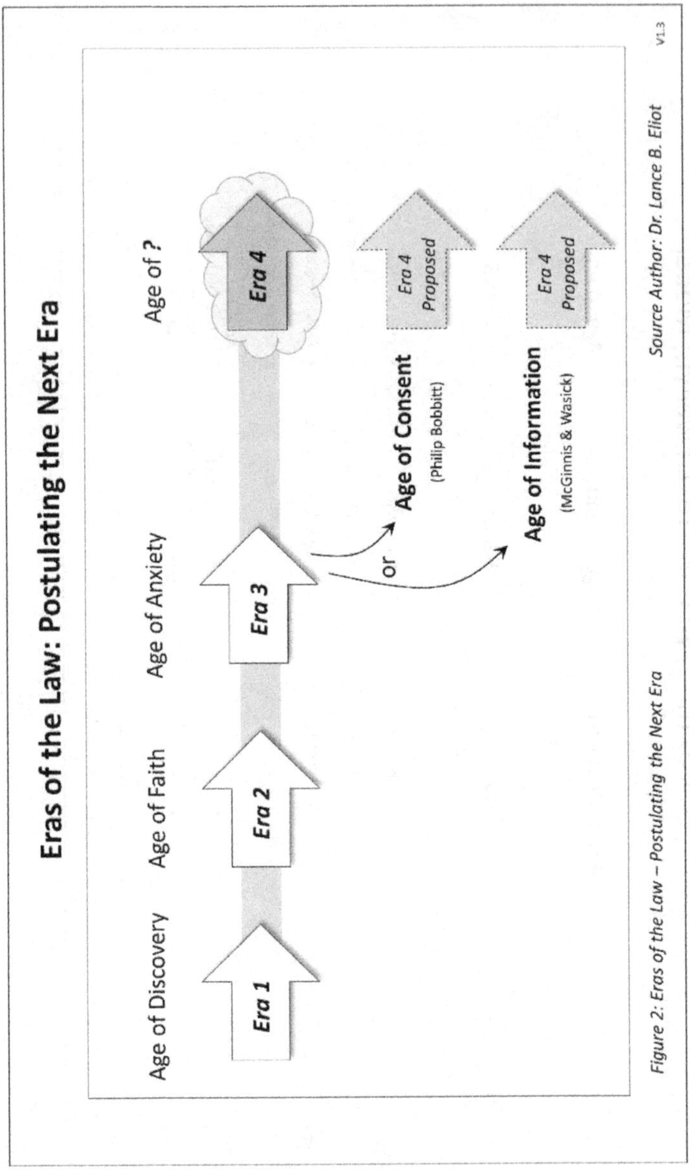
Eras of the Law: Postulating the Next Era
Age of Discovery
Age of Faith
Age of Anxiety
Age of ?
Era 1
Era 2
Era 3
Era 4
or
Age of Consent
(Philip Bobbitt)
Era 4 Proposed
Age of Information
(McGinnis & Wasick)
Era 4 Proposed
Figure 2: Eras of the Law – Postulating the Next Era
Source Author: Dr. Lance B. Eliot
V1.3

Figure 19

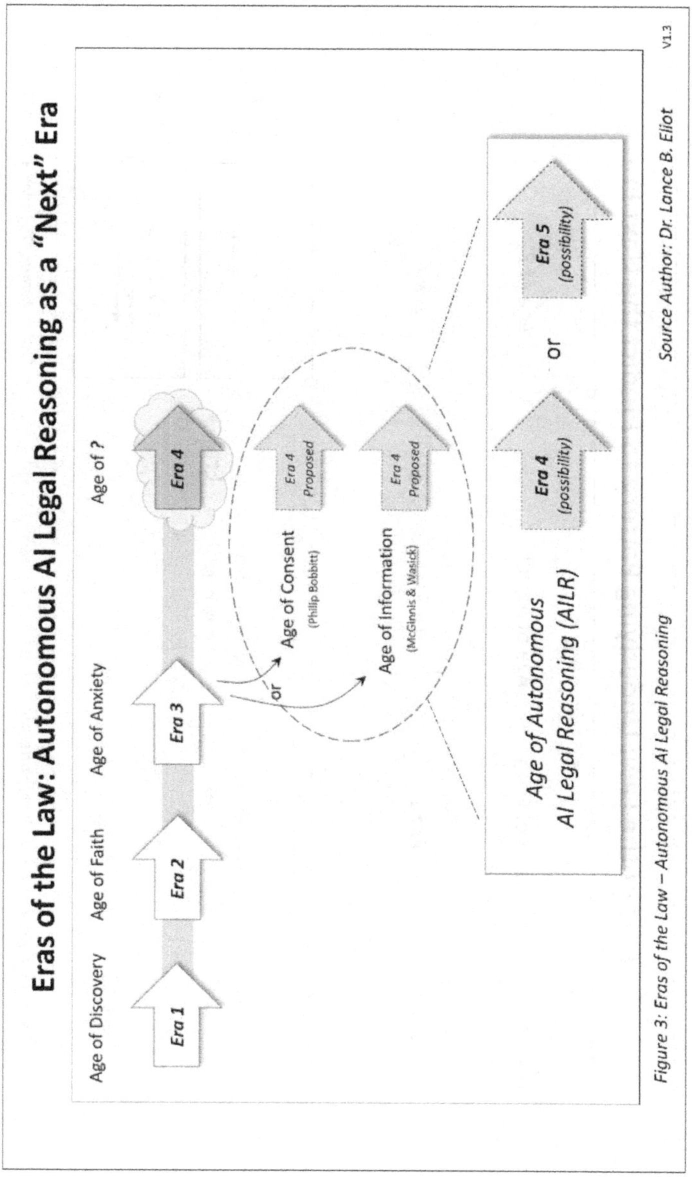
Eras of the Law: Autonomous AI Legal Reasoning as a "Next" Era
Age of Discovery
Age of Faith
Age of Anxiety
Age of ?
Era 1
Era 2
Era 3
Era 4
or
Age of Consent
(Philip Bobbitt)
Era 4 Proposed
Age of Information
(McGinnis & Wasick)
Era 4 Proposed
Age of Autonomous AI Legal Reasoning (AILR)
Era 4 (possibility)
or
Era 5 (possibility)
Figure 3: Eras of the Law – Autonomous AI Legal Reasoning
Source Author: Dr. Lance B. Eliot
V1.3

Figure 20

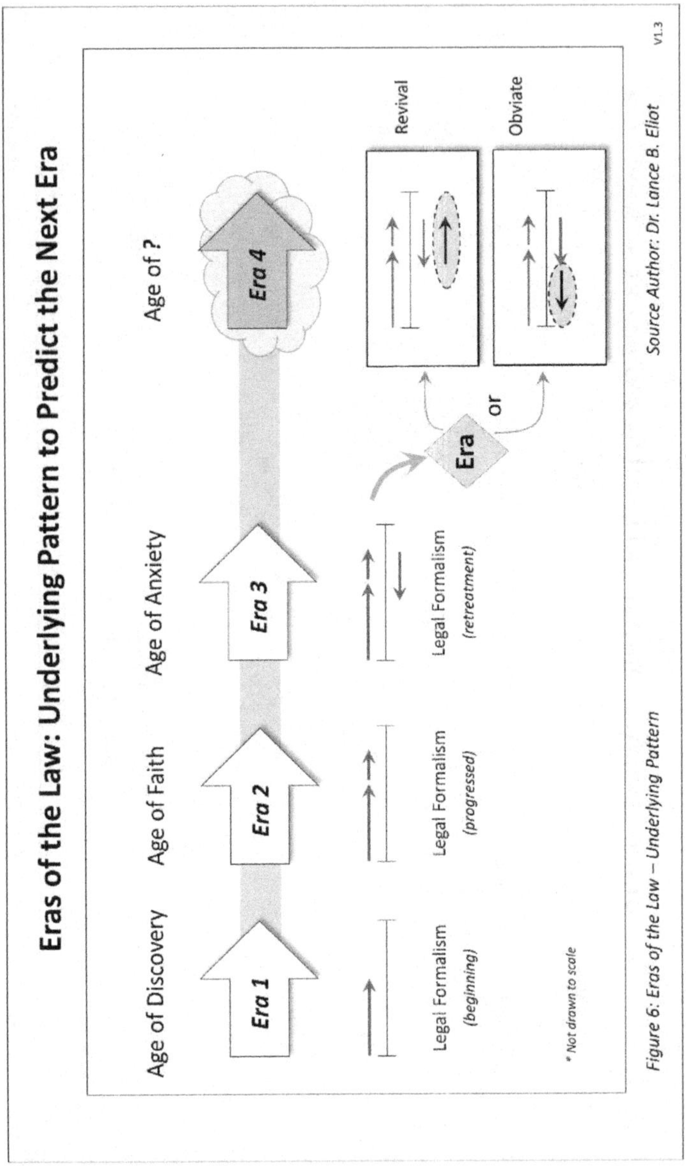
Eras of the Law: Underlying Pattern to Predict the Next Era
Age of Discovery
Age of Faith
Age of Anxiety
Age of ?
Era 1
Era 2
Era 3
Era 4
Legal Formalism
(beginning)
Legal Formalism
(progressed)
Legal Formalism
(retreatment)
* Not drawn to scale
Era
or
Revival
Obviate
Figure 6: Eras of the Law – Underlying Pattern
Source Author: Dr. Lance B. Eliot
V1.3

Figure 21

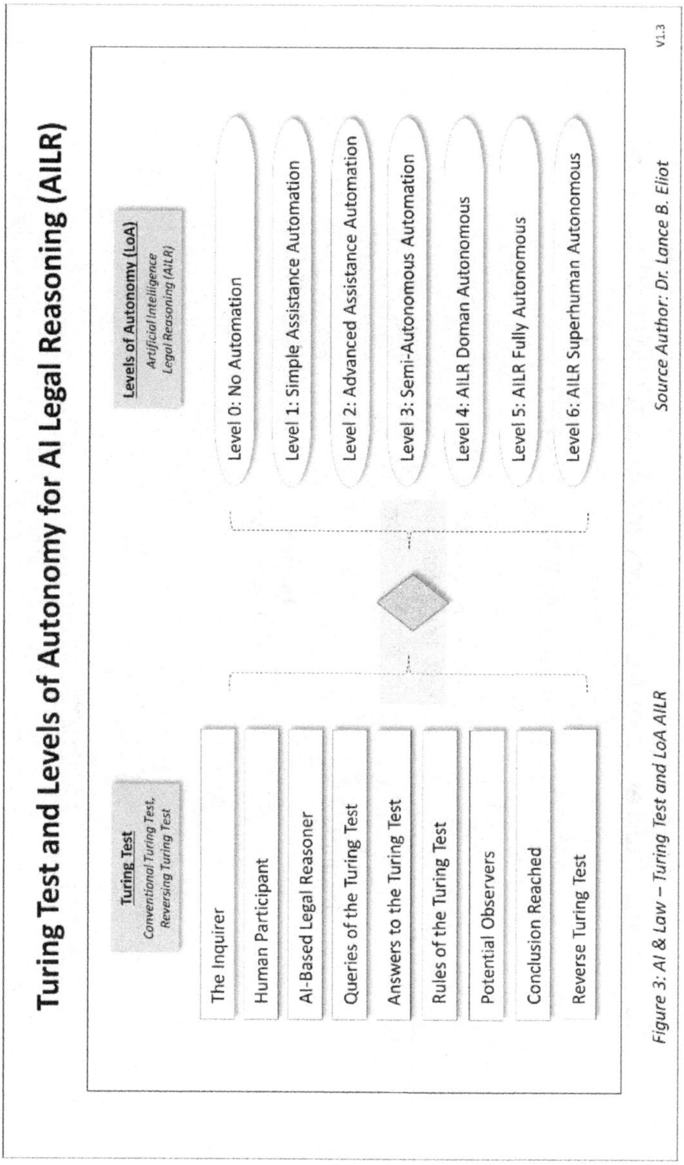
Turing Test and Levels of Autonomy for AI Legal Reasoning (AILR)
Turing Test
Conventional Turing Test,
Reversing Turing Test
Levels of Autonomy (LoA)
Artificial Intelligence
Legal Reasoning (AILR)
The Inquirer
Human Participant
AI-Based Legal Reasoner
Queries of the Turing Test
Answers to the Turing Test
Rules of the Turing Test
Potential Observers
Conclusion Reached
Reverse Turing Test
Level 0: No Automation
Level 1: Simple Assistance Automation
Level 2: Advanced Assistance Automation
Level 3: Semi-Autonomous Automation
Level 4: AILR Doman Autonomous
Level 5: AILR Fully Autonomous
Level 6: AILR Superhuman Autonomous
Figure 3: AI & Law – Turing Test and LoA AILR
Source Author: Dr. Lance B. Eliot
V1.3

Figure 22

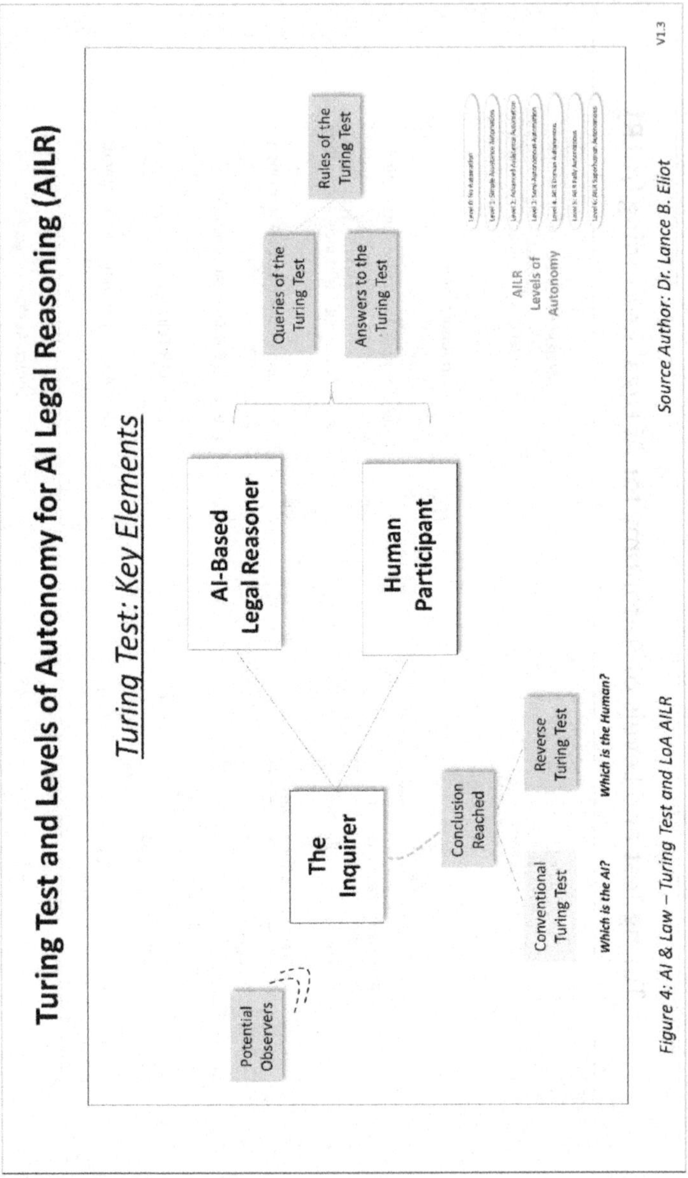
Turing Test and Levels of Autonomy for AI Legal Reasoning (AILR)
Turing Test: Key Elements
Potential Observers
The Inquirer
AI-Based Legal Reasoner
Human Participant
Queries of the Turing Test
Rules of the Turing Test
Answers to the Turing Test
Conclusion Reached
Conventional Turing Test
Reverse Turing Test
Which is the AI?
Which is the Human?
AILR Levels of Autonomy
Figure 4: AI & Law – Turing Test and LoA AILR
Source Author: Dr. Lance B. Eliot
V1.3

Figure 23

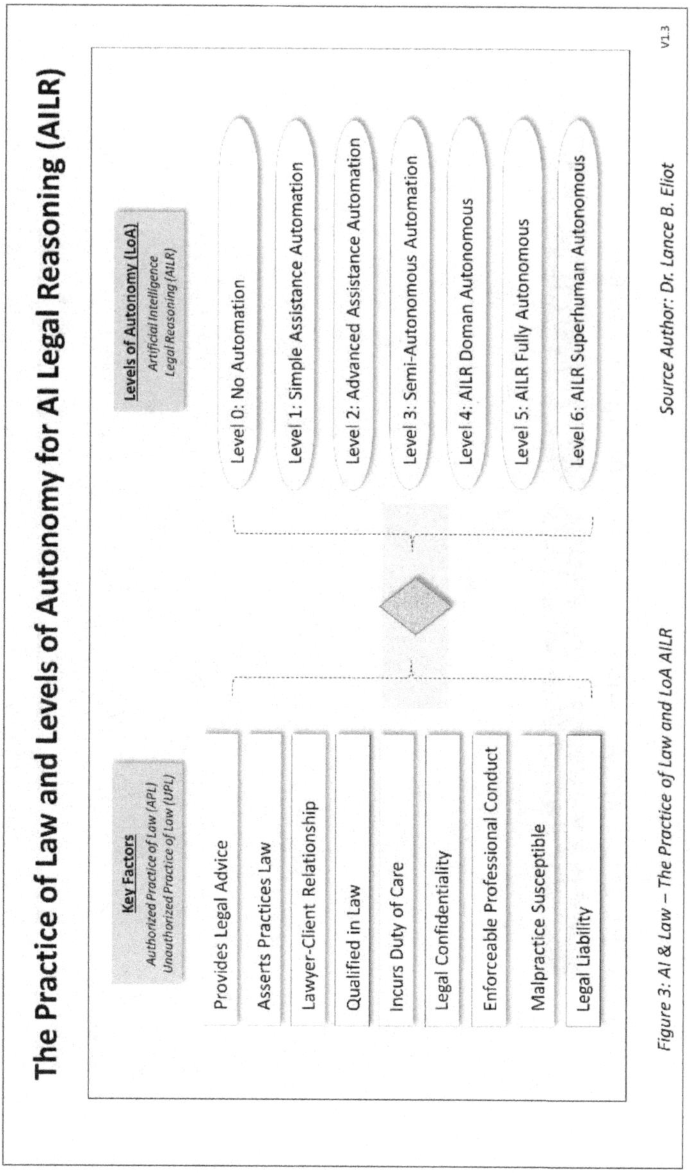

Figure 3: AI & Law – The Practice of Law and LoA AILR

Figure 24

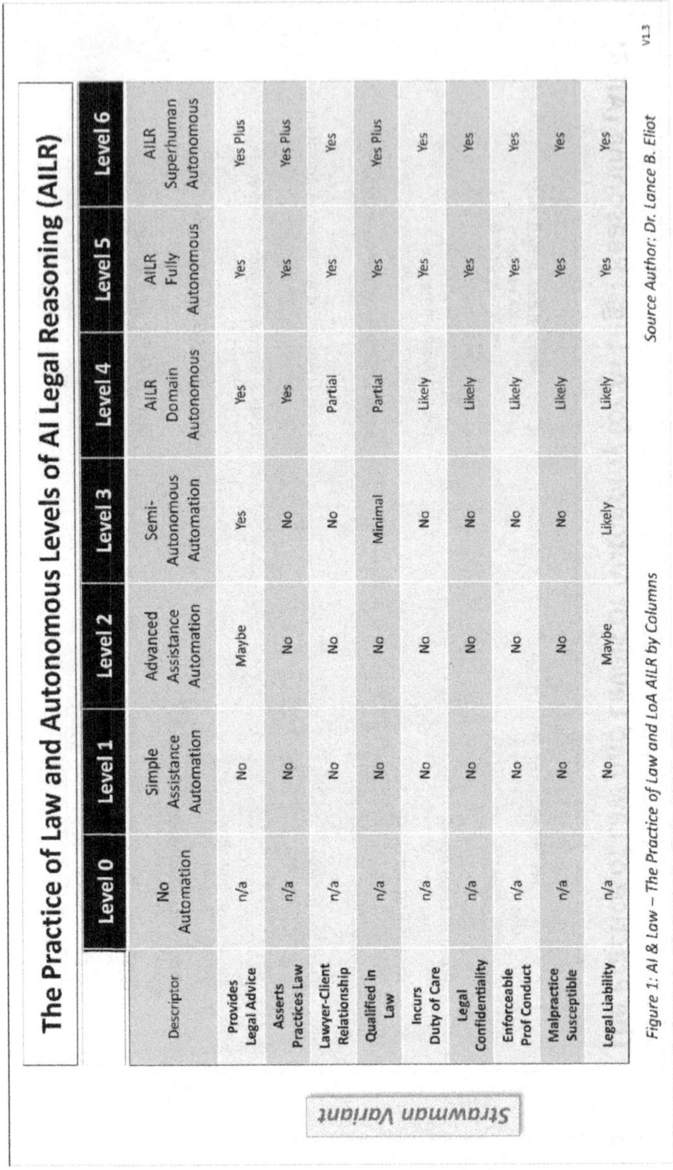

The Practice of Law and Autonomous Levels of AI Legal Reasoning (AILR)

Descriptor	Level 0	Level 1	Level 2	Level 3	Level 4	Level 5	Level 6
	No Automation	Simple Assistance Automation	Advanced Assistance Automation	Semi-Autonomous Automation	AILR Domain Autonomous	AILR Fully Autonomous	AILR Superhuman Autonomous
Provides Legal Advice	n/a	No	Maybe	Yes	Yes	Yes	Yes Plus
Asserts Practices Law	n/a	No	No	No	Yes	Yes	Yes Plus
Lawyer-Client Relationship	n/a	No	No	No	Partial	Yes	Yes
Qualified in Law	n/a	No	No	Minimal	Partial	Yes	Yes Plus
Incurs Duty of Care	n/a	No	No	No	Likely	Yes	Yes
Legal Confidentiality	n/a	No	No	No	Likely	Yes	Yes
Enforceable Prof Conduct	n/a	No	No	No	Likely	Yes	Yes
Malpractice Susceptible	n/a	No	No	No	Likely	Yes	Yes
Legal Liability	n/a	No	Maybe	Likely	Likely	Yes	Yes

Figure 1: AI & Law – The Practice of Law and LoA AILR by Columns

Source Author: Dr. Lance B. Eliot

V13

Strawman Variant

Figure 25

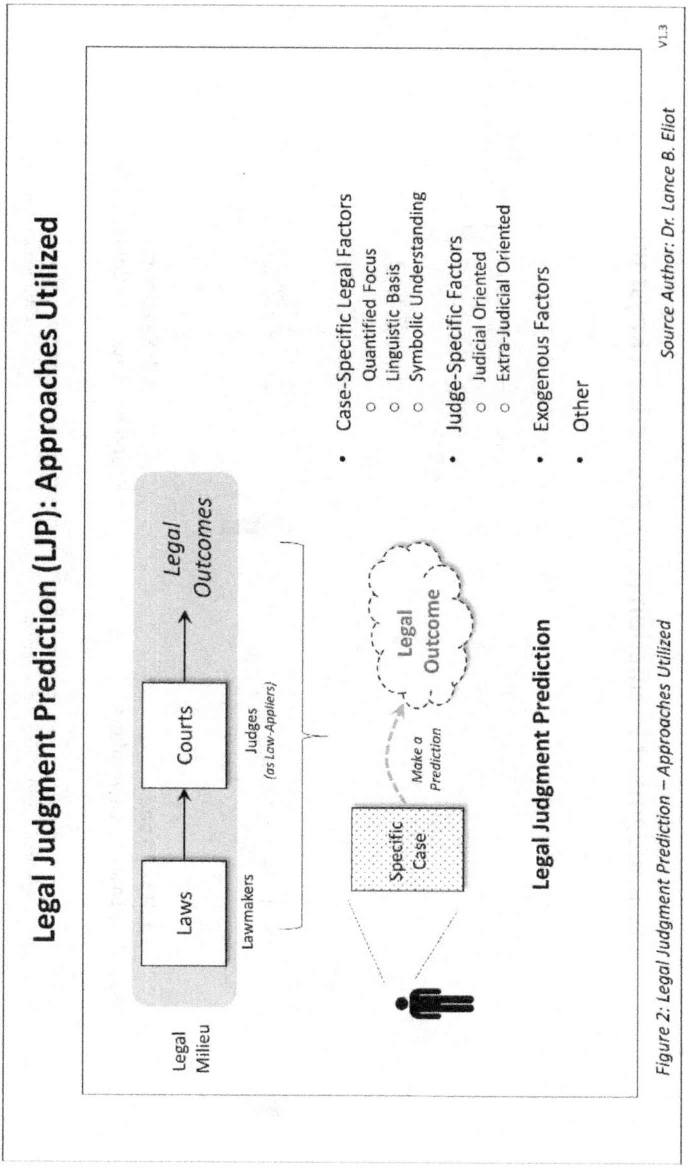
Legal Judgment Prediction (LJP): Approaches Utilized
Legal Milieu
Laws
Courts
Legal Outcomes
Lawmakers
Judges
(as Law-Appliers)
Specific Case
Make a Prediction
Legal Outcome
Legal Judgment Prediction
• Case-Specific Legal Factors
○ Quantified Focus
○ Linguistic Basis
○ Symbolic Understanding
• Judge-Specific Factors
○ Judicial Oriented
○ Extra-Judicial Oriented
• Exogenous Factors
• Other
Figure 2: Legal Judgment Prediction – Approaches Utilized
Source Author: Dr. Lance B. Eliot
V1.3

Figure 26

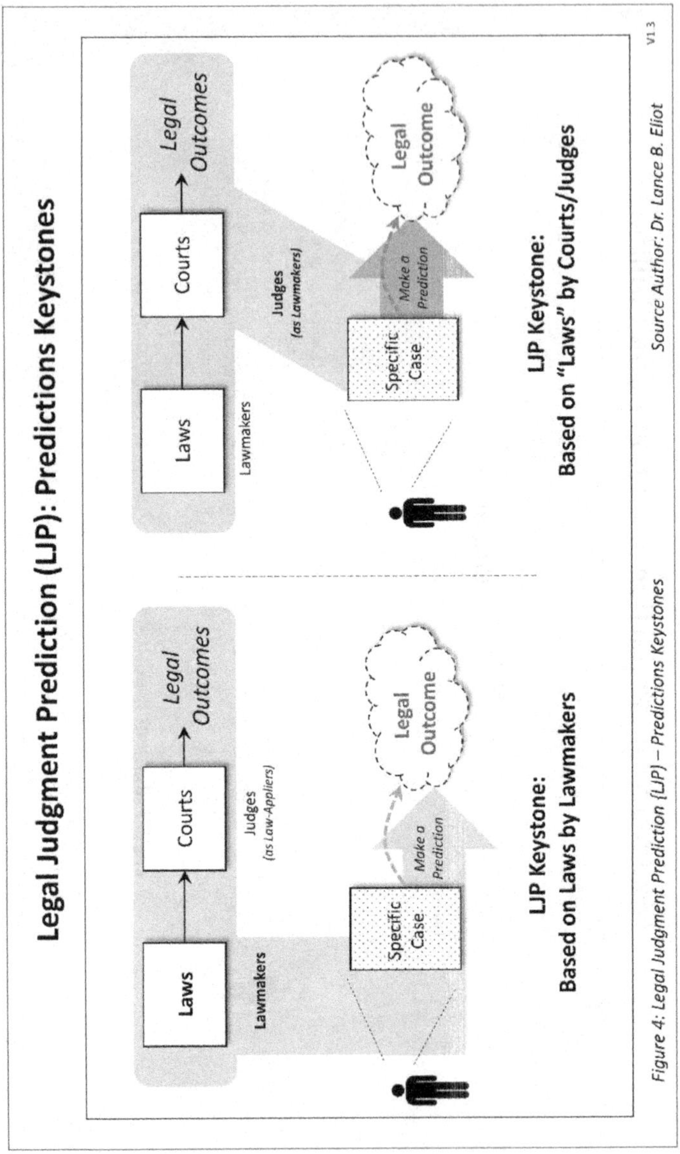
Legal Judgment Prediction (LJP): Predictions Keystones
Laws
Courts
Legal Outcomes
Lawmakers
Judges (as Law-Appliers)
Specific Case
Make a Prediction
Legal Outcome
LJP Keystone: Based on Laws by Lawmakers
Judges (as Lawmakers)
LJP Keystone: Based on "Laws" by Courts/Judges
Figure 4: Legal Judgment Prediction (LJP) – Predictions Keystones
Source Author: Dr. Lance B. Eliot
V1.3

Figure 27

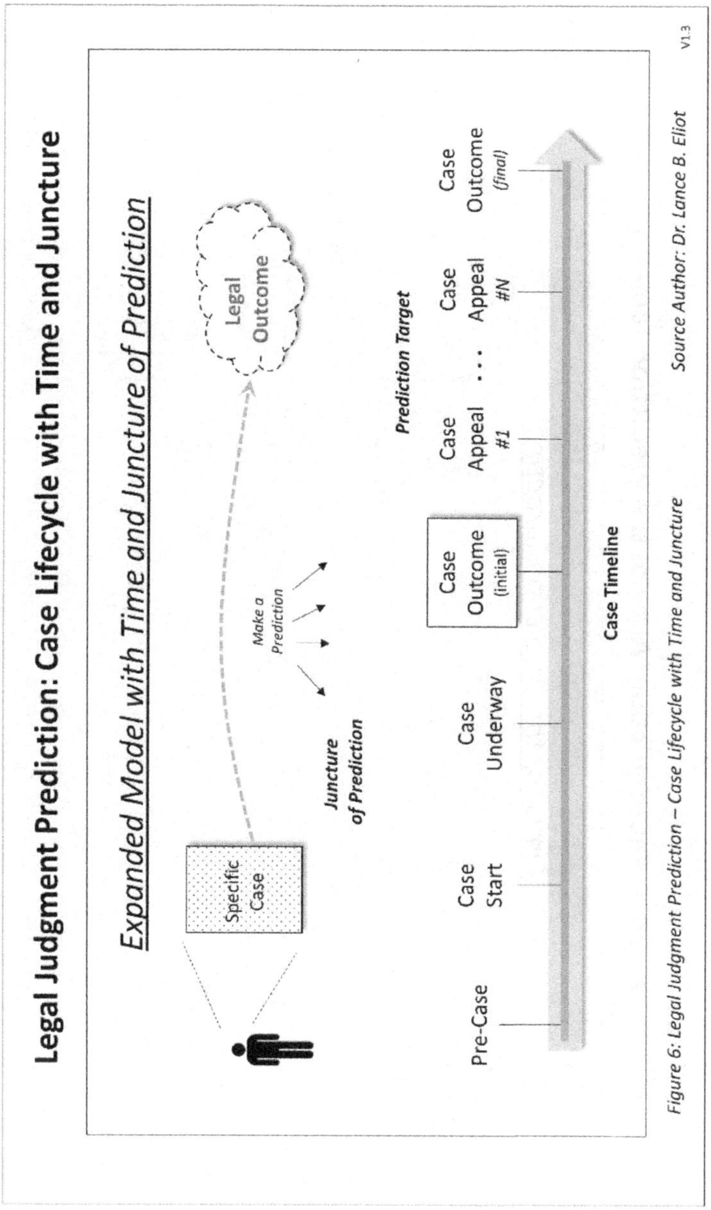
Legal Judgment Prediction: Case Lifecycle with Time and Juncture
Expanded Model with Time and Juncture of Prediction
Specific Case
Legal Outcome
Make a Prediction
Juncture of Prediction
Prediction Target
Pre-Case
Case Start
Case Underway
Case Outcome (initial)
Case Appeal #1
. . .
Case Appeal #N
Case Outcome (final)
Case Timeline
Figure 6: Legal Judgment Prediction – Case Lifecycle with Time and Juncture
Source Author: Dr. Lance B. Eliot
V1.3

Figure 28

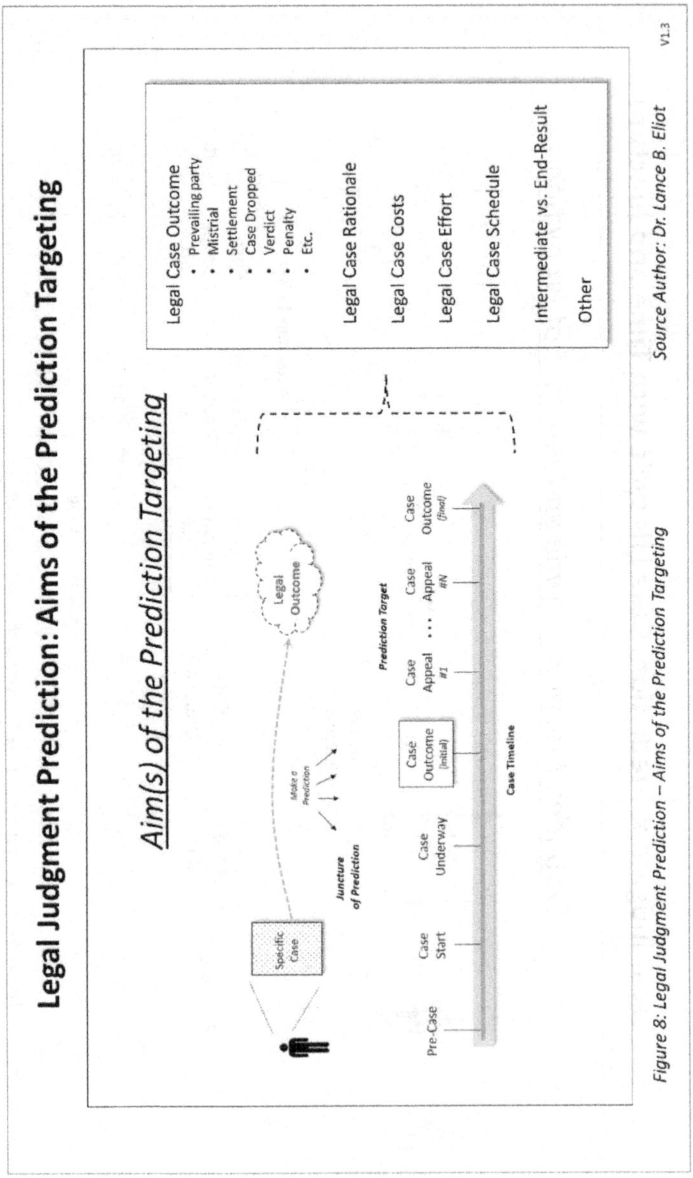

Legal Judgment Prediction: Aims of the Prediction Targeting
Aim(s) of the Prediction Targeting
Specific Case
Juncture of Prediction
Make a Prediction
Legal Outcome
Prediction Target
Pre-Case
Case Start
Case Underway
Case Outcome (initial)
Case Appeal #1
. . .
Case Appeal #N
Case Outcome (final)
Case Timeline
Legal Case Outcome
Prevailing party
Mistrial
Settlement
Case Dropped
Verdict
Penalty
Etc.
Legal Case Rationale
Legal Case Costs
Legal Case Effort
Legal Case Schedule
Intermediate vs. End-Result
Other
Figure 8: Legal Judgment Prediction – Aims of the Prediction Targeting
Source Author: Dr. Lance B. Eliot
V1.3

Figure 29

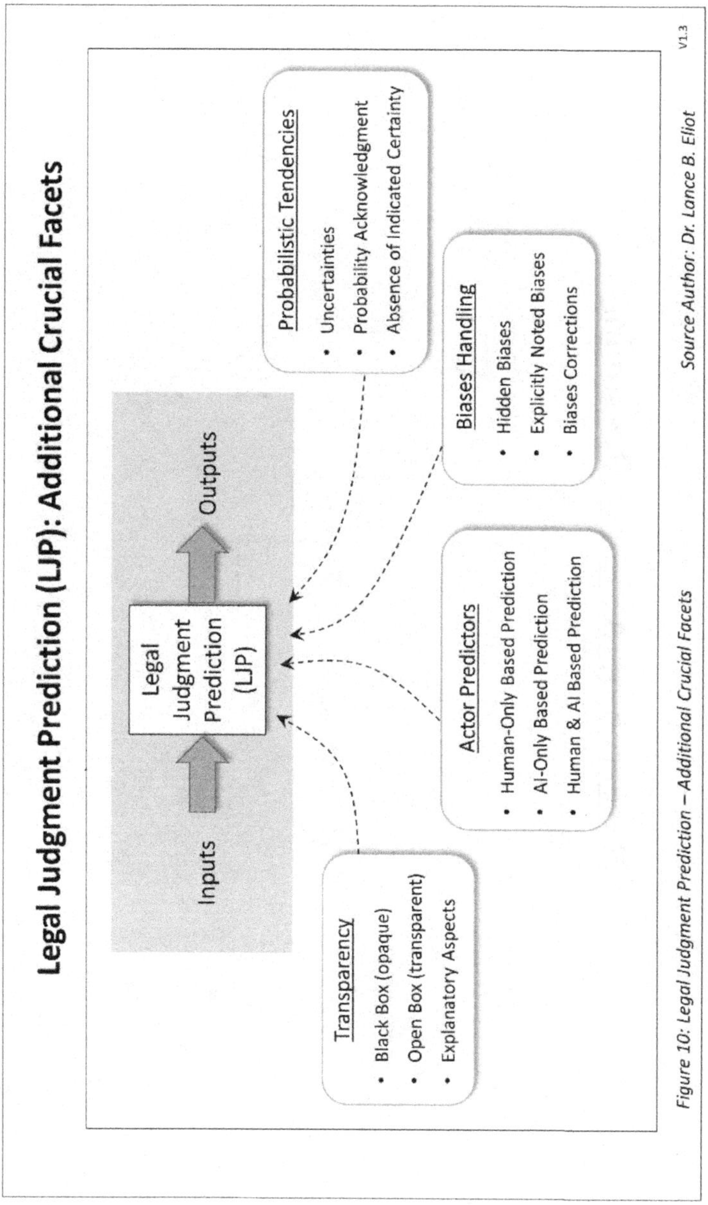
Legal Judgment Prediction (LJP): Additional Crucial Facets
Inputs
Legal Judgment Prediction (LJP)
Outputs
Transparency
Black Box (opaque)
Open Box (transparent)
Explanatory Aspects
Actor Predictors
Human-Only Based Prediction
AI-Only Based Prediction
Human & AI Based Prediction
Biases Handling
Hidden Biases
Explicitly Noted Biases
Biases Corrections
Probabilistic Tendencies
Uncertainties
Probability Acknowledgment
Absence of Indicated Certainty
Figure 10: Legal Judgment Prediction – Additional Crucial Facets
Source Author: Dr. Lance B. Eliot
V1.3

Figure 30

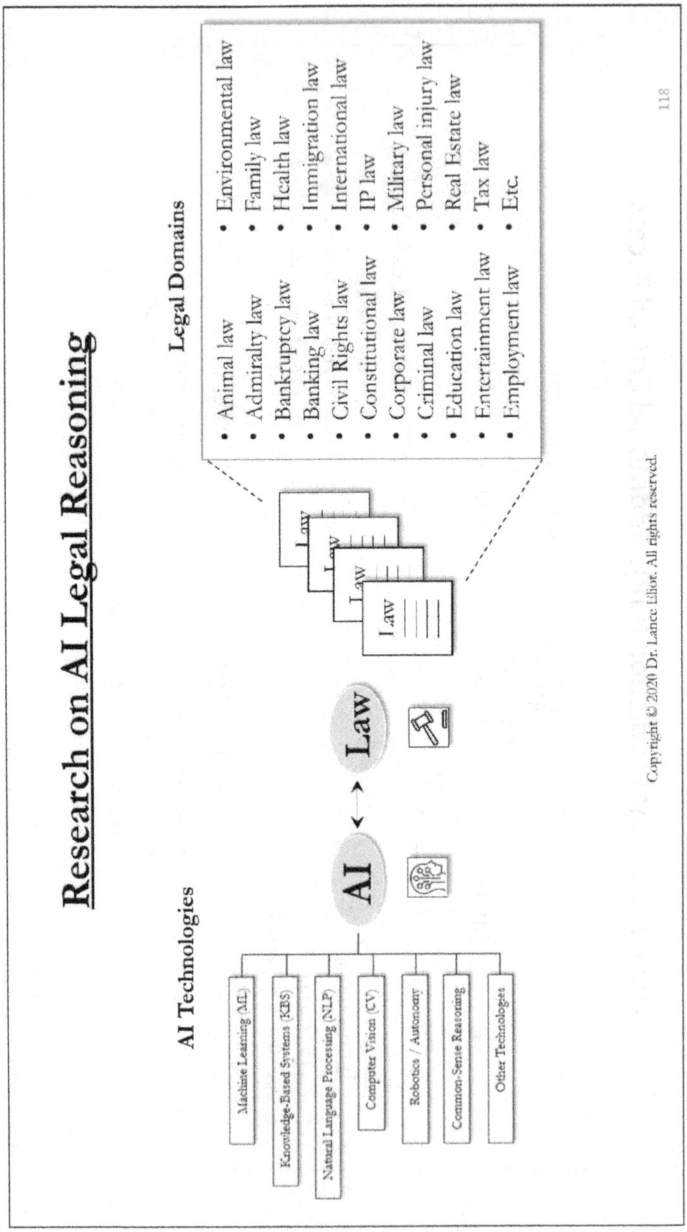
Research on AI Legal Reasoning
AI Technologies
Machine Learning (ML)
Knowledge-Based Systems (KBS)
Natural Language Processing (NLP)
Computer Vision (CV)
Robotics / Autonomy
Common-Sense Reasoning
Other Technologies
AI
Law
Law
Law
Law
Law
Legal Domains
• Animal law
• Admiralty law
• Bankruptcy law
• Banking law
• Civil Rights law
• Constitutional law
• Corporate law
• Criminal law
• Education law
• Entertainment law
• Employment law
• Environmental law
• Family law
• Health law
• Immigration law
• International law
• IP law
• Military law
• Personal injury law
• Real Estate law
• Tax law
• Etc.
Copyright © 2020 Dr. Lance Eliot. All rights reserved.
118

Figure 31

Companion Book By Dr. Lance Eliot

"Artificial Intelligence and Legal Reasoning Essentials"

ISBN 978-1-73460165-7

Chapters

<u>Companion Book By Dr. Lance Eliot</u>

"Artificial Intelligence and LegalTech Essentials"

ISBN 978-1-7346016-3-3

Chapters

<u>Companion Book By Dr. Lance Eliot</u>

"Decisive Essays On AI And Law"

ISBN 978-1-73630310-8

Chapters

Available on Amazon and via other online book sellers

Companion Book By Dr. Lance Eliot

"Incisive Research On AI And Law"

ISBN 978-1-73630311-5

Chapters

Available on Amazon and via other online book sellers

Companion Book By Dr. Lance Eliot

"Ingenious Essays On AI And Law"

ISBN 978-1-73630312-2

Chapters

Available on Amazon and via other online book seller

Companion Book By Dr. Lance Eliot

"Compelling Essays On AI And Law"

ISBN 978-1-73630313-9

Chapters

Available on Amazon and via other online book sellers

Companion Book By Dr. Lance Eliot

"Topnotch Essays On AI And Law"

ISBN 978-1-73630314-6

Chapters

Available on Amazon and via other online book sellers

Companion Book By Dr. Lance Eliot

"Trendsetting Essays On AI And Law"

ISBN 978-1-95-738601-0

Chapters

Available on Amazon and via other online book sellers

Companion Book By Dr. Lance Eliot

"Trailblazing Essays On AI And Law"

ISBN 978-1-95-738602-7

Chapters

Available on Amazon and via other online book sellers

Companion Book By Dr. Lance Eliot

"Leading Edge Essays On AI And Law"

ISBN 978-1-95-738604-1

Chapters

Available on Amazon and via other online book sellers

Companion Book By Dr. Lance Eliot

"Jurisprudent Essays On AI And Law"

ISBN 978-1-95-738604-1

Chapters

Available on Amazon and via other online book sellers

Companion Book By Dr. Lance Eliot

"AI And Law Amid Ethical AI Trends"

ISBN 978-1-95-738607-2

Chapters

ABOUT THE AUTHOR

Dr. Lance B. Eliot, Ph.D., MBA is a globally recognized AI expert and thought leader, an invited Stanford Fellow at Stanford University, an experienced top executive and corporate leader, a successful entrepreneur, and a noted scholar on AI, including that his Forbes and AI Trends columns have amassed over 4 million views, his books on AI are ranked in the Top 10 of all-time AI books, his journal articles are widely cited, and he has developed and implemented numerous AI systems.

He currently serves as the Chief AI Scientist at Techbruim, Inc. and has over twenty years of industry experience including serving as a corporate officer in billion-dollar sized firms and was a partner in a major consulting firm. He is also a successful entrepreneur having founded, ran, and sold several high-tech related businesses.

Dr. Eliot previously hosted the popular radio show *Technotrends* that was also available on American Airlines flights via their in-flight audio program, he has made appearances on CNN, has been a frequent speaker at industry conferences, and his podcasts have been downloaded over 150,000 times.

A former professor at the University of Southern California (USC), he founded and led an innovative research lab on Artificial Intelligence. He also previously served on the faculty of the University of California Los Angeles (UCLA) and was a visiting professor at other major universities. He was elected to the International Board of the Society for Information Management (SIM), a prestigious association of over 3,000 high-tech executives worldwide.

He has performed extensive community service, including serving as Senior Science Adviser to the Congressional Vice-Chair of the Congressional Committee on Science & Technology. He has served on the Board of the OC Science & Engineering Fair (OCSEF), where he is also has been a Grand Sweepstakes judge, and likewise served as a judge for the Intel International SEF (ISEF). He served as the Vice-Chair of the Association for Computing Machinery (ACM) Chapter, a prestigious association of computer scientists. Dr. Eliot has been a shark tank judge for the USC Mark Stevens Center for Innovation on start-up pitch competitions and served as a mentor for several incubators and accelerators in Silicon Valley and in Silicon Beach.

Dr. Eliot holds a Ph.D. from USC, MBA, and Bachelor's in Computer Science, and earned the CDP, CCP, CSP, CDE, and CISA certification.

ADDENDUM

Thanks for reading this book and I hope you will continue your interest in the field of AI & Law

---

For my free podcasts about AI & Law:

https://ai-law.libsyn.com/website

Those podcasts are also available on Spotify, iTunes, etc.

For the latest on AI & Law see my website:

www.ai-law.legal

To follow me on Twitter:

https://twitter.com/LanceEliot

For my in-depth book on AI & Law:

AI And Legal Reasoning Essentials

www.amazon.com/gp/product/1734601655/

Made in the USA
Monee, IL
05 November 2026

67808594R00154